絵で覚えるひらがな・カタカナ 改訂版

KANA
CAN BE EASY

[Revised Edition] Kunihiko Ogawa

the japan times PUBLISHING

Kana Can Be Easy [Revised Edition] 絵で覚えるひらがな・カタカナ [改訂版]

1990年 5月20日　初版発行
2016年12月20日　第2版発行
2024年10月20日　第5刷発行
著　者：小川邦彦
発行者：伊藤秀樹
発行所：株式会社 ジャパンタイムズ出版
　　　　〒102-0082 東京都千代田区一番町2-2
　　　　一番町第二TGビル2F
ISBN978-4-7890-1661-2

Originally published in 1975 as a service to the faculty and students of San Diego State University.
Copyright © 1975 by Kunihiko Ogawa

Copyright © 1990 & 2016 by Kunihiko Ogawa

All rights reserved. No part of this publication may be reproduced, stored in a retrieval system, or transmitted in any form or by any means, electronic, mechanical, photocopying, recording, or otherwise, without the prior written permission of the publisher.

First edition: May 1990
Second edition: December 2016
5th printing: October 2024

Illustrations: Noriko Udagawa
Layout design and typesetting: DEP, Inc.
Cover art: tobufune (Shohei Oguchi / Nanako Uebo / Kaho Iwanaga)
Printing: Nikkei Printing Inc.

Published by The Japan Times Publishing, Ltd.
2F Ichibancho Daini TG Bldg., 2-2 Ichibancho, Chiyoda-ku, Tokyo 102-0082, Japan
Website: https://jtpublishing.co.jp/

ISBN978-4-7890-1661-2

Printed in Japan

Preface

It is well-known that the Japanese writing system, among those of the world languages, is uniquely complex. It involves *kanji* (Chinese characters), *hiragana* and *katakana* (the two types of the Japanese syllabaries), and *rōmaji* (the Roman alphabet). To those learning the language, this complex writing system is indeed a serious liability which cannot be avoided.

This book is intended to ease the burden for beginning learners by introducing the two types of the Japanese syllabaries, *hiragana* and *katakana*, through a method which is intended to assist in memorizing, recognizing and producing each character of the *kana* (syllabaries) through pictorial association. For example, the *hiragana* "*ku*" or く happens to be shaped like the widely opened bill of, say, a *cuckoo*; thus the shape and sound of the *hiragana* "*ku*" can be easily connected to each other through the picture of a cuckoo.

Early mastery of the *kana* is an unavoidable necessity. It is the author's sincere hope that this book will minimize the learners' time and mental fatigue in learning the *kana* and will rather make this learning experience, which is otherwise somewhat tedious, quick and fun.

This book is the completely modified version of my *Mnemonic Aids to the Japanese Syllabaries*, which was published by San Diego State University in 1975. I am indebted to Conan Grames, with whom I taught Japanese at the University of Utah, for inspiring some of the original ideas.

Special thanks are due to Fujiko Motohashi for her many helpful comments and suggestions. Thanks also go to Jackie Rives for her sound advice. I am especially grateful to Chiaki Kaku for her inestimable assistance in the editing of this manuscript.

Kunihiko Ogawa
Kofu, Japan
May 1990

(This preface was written
for the first edition.)

Contents

Preface 3
How to Use This Book 6

Introduction ——————————————————————— 8
- *Hiragana* and *Rōmaji* 10
- *Katakana* and *Rōmaji* 11

Hiragana ——————————————————————— 13

Katakana ——————————————————————— 61

Appendix ——————————————————————— 109
   I. Elaborations of Basic *Hiragana* and *Katakana* 110
   II. Punctuation Marks 115

Practices ——————————————————————— 117
- *Hiragana* Practice 1–5 117–121
- *Katakana* Practice 1–5 122–126
- Answers 127–128

How to Use This Book

A | *Kana* and the picture

1. On each page, the large picture in the upper right-hand corner ① is designed to help you associate the sound and shape of the Japanese syllabary systems (*kana*, or *hiragana* and *katakana*). Look at the picture and read the caption ②, trying to associate the picture with the crucial sound indicated in boldface in the underlined word. The crucial sound in the caption is intended as a helpful approximation to the proper reading of each *kana*.
2. Spend a few minutes until you can visualize the picture and its accompanying caption in your head.
3. Compare the picture with the corresponding *kana* to the left of it ③. Pay attention to every detail of the model *kana*.
4. Cover the *kana* with your hand, and look at the picture again. Do this until you can visualize the *kana* clearly in the picture.

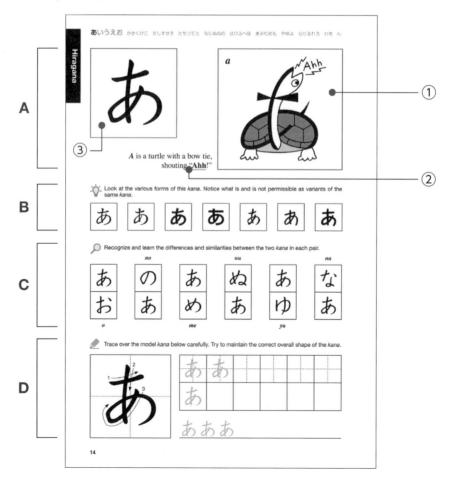

5. Next, cover the picture with your hand, and keep looking at the *kana* until you can visualize the picture in the *kana*.
6. Now cover both the picture and the caption with your hand(s), and keep looking at the *kana* until you can visualize the picture and recall the crucial sound in the caption.

B | Variants of *kana*

Next, look at the alternative examples of the *kana*. You may see these various forms in Japanese publications and writing.

C | Distinguishing from other *kana*

Then look at the pairs of *kana* in the center of the page. Notice the differences and similarities between the *kana* in question and the other paired with it. Some differences which may look trivial to you are very significant in differentiating *kana*. On the other hand, there are some insignificant differences among variants of the same *kana* which may look important to you.
- When *katakana* is displayed in this part of the *hiragana* pages, its reading is provided in ( ), or vice versa.

D | Writing practice

Now trace over the model *kana* in gray and fill in all the remaining boxes and spaces on the line with the same *kana*. Take care to maintain the correct overall shape. When writing in a box, make sure to center the *kana* in each box, not too big or not too small for the box. Write very deliberately; common mistakes are hurrying too much, drawing meaningless lines, omitting important lines, and curving, slanting, or straightening lines in the wrong manner. Never scribble.

- Repeat this process for each page.
- After every ten pages, test your memory of the *kana* you have learned. You can use practice sheets provided at the back of the book.
- Before proceeding to the *katakana* section, review the total *hiragana* section completely. The thorough mastery of *hiragana* will make it easy to learn *katakana* because many *katakana* resemble the corresponding *hiragana*.

Introduction

What is *kana*?

Until about the fifth century A.D., Japan had no writing system of its own. Then, the introduction of *kanji*, as Chinese characters are called in Japan, made it possible to write the Japanese language. Although Chinese characters had their own original particular Chinese sounds and meanings, they were mainly adapted to Japanese as *kanji* by selecting only those characters whose Chinese meanings matched or approximated those of the Japanese language.

Because there were many cases where Japanese grammar was different from Chinese so that no Chinese characters exactly corresponded to the meanings of Japanese (for example, particles, verb and adjective endings), some *kanji* were used merely as phonetic signs or syllabaries representing Japanese sounds without regard to their original Chinese meanings. The number of such *kanji* was gradually narrowed down to some fifty, the minimum number which can represent Japanese syllables. Eventually the Japanese syllabaries called *hiragana* and *katakana* replaced such *kanji*.

It is said that *hiragana* were originated by a woman or women in the early Heian period (therefore, once called *onna moji*, or women's characters) on the basis of modifying the shape of *kanji* so as to be written quickly in a cursive, flowing style without lifting the brush. *Katakana* were developed by many people including Buddhist monks also in the Heian period on the basis of adopting just one portion of *kanji*, rather than the entire shape. For example, see the following:

	Kanji	Hiragana	Katakana
"na"	奈	な	ナ

The *hiragana* "na" is a simplified, modified form of the entire corresponding *kanji* "na," while the *katakana* "na" consists only of the upper left of the corresponding *kanji*.

Much later in the sixteenth century, European missionaries started to come to Japan. They introduced the Roman alphabet or *rōmaji* to Japan. Since then, Japanese can be represented entirely by *rōmaji* if necessary.

The current Japanese writing system

Japanese sentences can be written vertically, top to bottom, right to left. The front pages of newspapers and books published in Japanese start on the opposite side of those published in English. Some books and scientific papers and documents containing Arabic numerals, formulas and foreign words are usually written horizontally, left to right, like those published in English. There is no special spacing between words in a sentence unlike English, but punctuation marks such as commas and periods (small circles in Japanese) are used in Japanese.

Kanji, *hiragana* and *katakana* are used in ordinary writing. Usually, though not strictly mandatorily, *kanji* are used for expressing "meaningful" elements such as nouns and stems of adjectives and verbs. *Hiragana* are used for expressing "grammatical" elements such as particles, and endings of adjectives and verbs which show tenses, etc. *Katakana* are usually reserved for loan words borrowed from Indo-European languages (e.g., "television", "radio"). In addition, *rōmaji* may also be used to write Japanese. Its use is generally confined to names of train stations, stores, companies, modern store merchandise and the like. This is often intended for the convenience of foreigners in Japan or as a kind of fashionable decoration.

It is possible to write an entire Japanese sentence in *hiragana*. If an adult forgets certain *kanji* which are rarely used, he may substitute *hiragana* for them. Since the basic 46 *hiragana* symbols and some modifications of them suffice for all Japanese sounds, Japanese children start to read and write Japanese all in *hiragana* before making an attempt to learn the some two thousand *kanji* currently used.

Kana, *rōmaji* and the Japanese syllables

If you agree that Spanish is an easy language to pronounce, you will also admit that Japanese pronunciation presents very few problems to most foreign students. Thus *rōmaji*, which are not rigid phonetic signs, can function as convenient representation of Japanese for those whose languages make use of the Roman alphabet.

Japanese has five vowels, thirteen consonants and two semi-vowels, all of which make up 104 syllables. Each combination stands for each syllable. It is these syllables that are represented by the *hiragana* and *katakana* syllabaries. Forty-six basic *hiragana*/*katakana* represent 46 syllables, and all the remaining syllables can be represented by these *hiragana*/*katakana* with slight modifications. The syllables are presented by the following chart in the order given in Japanese schools.

There are two Romanization systems: the conventional Hepburn System still widely used, and the official *Kunreishiki* System ("Official System") designated for use in Japanese schools. Between the two, Hepburn presents closer approximations to "real" sounds than *Kunreishiki*, though *Kunreishiki* has more uniformity in representation than Hepburn.

Hiragana and Rōmaji

Rōmaji in ( ) are written according to the *Kunreishiki* System.

Basic *hiragana*

あ	a	い	i	う	u	え	e	お	o
か	ka	き	ki	く	ku	け	ke	こ	ko
さ	sa	し	shi (si)	す	su	せ	se	そ	so
た	ta	ち	chi (ti)	つ	tsu (tu)	て	te	と	to
な	na	に	ni	ぬ	nu	ね	ne	の	no
は	ha	ひ	hi	ふ	fu (hu)	へ	he	ほ	ho
ま	ma	み	mi	む	mu	め	me	も	mo
や	ya			ゆ	yu			よ	yo
ら	ra	り	ri	る	ru	れ	re	ろ	ro
わ	wa							を	o
ん	n								

Hiragana with two dots / a little circle

が	ga	ぎ	gi	ぐ	gu	げ	ge	ご	go
ざ	za	じ	ji (zi)	ず	zu	ぜ	ze	ぞ	zo
だ	da	ぢ	ji (zi)	づ	zu	で	de	ど	do
ば	ba	び	bi	ぶ	bu	べ	be	ぼ	bo
ぱ	pa	ぴ	pi	ぷ	pu	ぺ	pe	ぽ	po

Hiragana with small や (ya) / ゆ (yu) / よ (yo)

きゃ	kya	きゅ	kyu	きょ	kyo
しゃ	sha (sya)	しゅ	shu (syu)	しょ	sho (syo)
ちゃ	cha (tya)	ちゅ	chu (tyu)	ちょ	cho (tyo)
にゃ	nya	にゅ	nyu	にょ	nyo
ひゃ	hya	ひゅ	hyu	ひょ	hyo
みゃ	mya	みゅ	myu	みょ	myo
りゃ	rya	りゅ	ryu	りょ	ryo
ぎゃ	gya	ぎゅ	gyu	ぎょ	gyo
じゃ	ja (zya)	じゅ	ju (zyu)	じょ	jo (zyo)
びゃ	bya	びゅ	byu	びょ	byo
ぴゃ	pya	ぴゅ	pyu	ぴょ	pyo

Katakana and Rōmaji

Rōmaji in ( ) are written according to the *Kunreishiki* System.

Basic katakana

ア	a	イ	i	ウ	u	エ	e	オ	o
カ	ka	キ	ki	ク	ku	ケ	ke	コ	ko
サ	sa	シ	shi (si)	ス	su	セ	se	ソ	so
タ	ta	チ	chi (ti)	ツ	tsu (tu)	テ	te	ト	to
ナ	na	ニ	ni	ヌ	nu	ネ	ne	ノ	no
ハ	ha	ヒ	hi	フ	fu (hu)	ヘ	he	ホ	ho
マ	ma	ミ	mi	ム	mu	メ	me	モ	mo
ヤ	ya			ユ	yu			ヨ	yo
ラ	ra	リ	ri	ル	ru	レ	re	ロ	ro
ワ	wa							ヲ	o
ン	n								

Katakana with two dots / a little circle

ガ	ga	ギ	gi	グ	gu	ゲ	ge	ゴ	go
ザ	za	ジ	ji (zi)	ズ	zu	ゼ	ze	ゾ	zo
ダ	da	ヂ	ji (zi)	ヅ	zu	デ	de	ド	do
バ	ba	ビ	bi	ブ	bu	ベ	be	ボ	bo
パ	pa	ピ	pi	プ	pu	ペ	pe	ポ	po

Katakana with small ヤ (ya) / ユ (yu) / ヨ (yo)

キャ	kya	キュ	kyu	キョ	kyo
シャ	sha (sya)	シュ	shu (syu)	ショ	sho (syo)
チャ	cha (tya)	チュ	chu (tyu)	チョ	cho (tyo)
ニャ	nya	ニュ	nyu	ニョ	nyo
ヒャ	hya	ヒュ	hyu	ヒョ	hyo
ミャ	mya	ミュ	myu	ミョ	myo
リャ	rya	リュ	ryu	リョ	ryo
ギャ	gya	ギュ	gyu	ギョ	gyo
ジャ	ja (zya)	ジュ	ju (zyu)	ジョ	jo (zyo)
ビャ	bya	ビュ	byu	ビョ	byo
ピャ	pya	ピュ	pyu	ピョ	pyo

Hiragana

As shown by the chart below, there are 46 basic *hiragana* characters representing 46 syllables. All the remaining syllables can be represented by these basic characters with slight modifications. Therefore, it is of great importance to master these 46 characters as early as possible in your study of Japanese. The modifications which are needed for the remaining syllables will be explained at the end of this book.

	a	i	u	e	o
	あ	い	う	え	お
k-	か	き	く	け	こ
s-	さ	し	す	せ	そ
t-	た	ち	つ	て	と
n-	な	に	ぬ	ね	の
h-	は	ひ	ふ	へ	ほ
m-	ま	み	む	め	も
y-	や		ゆ		よ
r-	ら	り	る	れ	ろ
w-	わ				を
n	ん				

あいうえお かきくけこ さしすせそ たちつてと なにぬねの はひふへほ まみむめも やゆよ らりるれろ わを ん

Hiragana

a

A is a turtle with a bow tie, shouting "**Ahh**!"

💡 Look at the various forms of this *kana*. Notice what is and is not permissible as variants of the same *kana*.

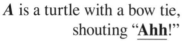

🔍 Recognize and learn the differences and similarities between the two *kana* in each pair.

	no		*nu*		*na*
o		*me*		*yu*	

✏️ Trace over the model *kana* below carefully. Try to maintain the correct overall shape of the *kana*.

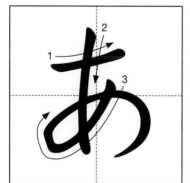

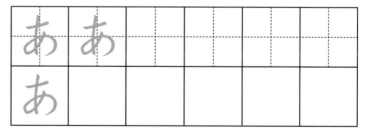

あいうえお　かきくけこ　さしすせそ　たちつてと　なにぬねの　はひふへほ　まみむめも　やゆよ　らりるれろ　わを　ん

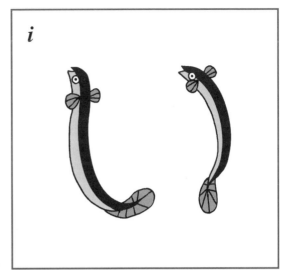

I is two **ee**ls.

💡 Look at the various forms of this *kana*. Notice what is and is not permissible as variants of the same *kana*.

🔍 Recognize and learn the differences and similarities between the two *kana* in each pair.

	ri		(*ru*)		(*ni*)
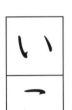		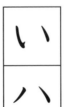			
ko	(*ha*)		(*so*)		

✏️ Trace over the model *kana* below carefully. Try to maintain the correct overall shape of the *kana*.

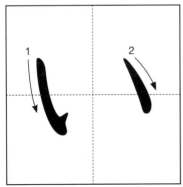
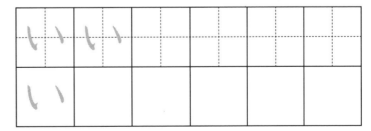

15

Hiragana

あいうえお かきくけこ さしすせそ たちつてと なにぬねの はひふへほ まみむめも やゆよ らりるれろ わを ん

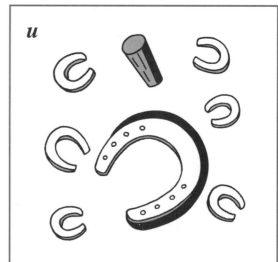

U is **oo**dles of horses**hoe**s tossed at a stake.

💡 Look at the various forms of this *kana*. Notice what is and is not permissible as variants of the same *kana*.

🔍 Recognize and learn the differences and similarities between the two *kana* in each pair.

                ra   (***u***)   (***ku***)

      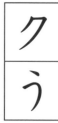

    (***ra***)   **tsu**   **ro**

✏️ Trace over the model *kana* below carefully. Try to maintain the correct overall shape of the *kana*.

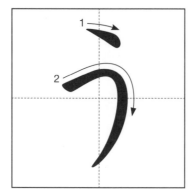

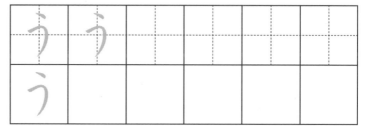

あいうえお かきくけこ さしすせそ たちつてと なにぬねの はひふへほ まみむめも やゆよ らりるれろ わを ん

E is an <u>e</u>lf.

💡 Look at the various forms of this *kana*. Notice what is and is not permissible as variants of the same *kana*.

🔍 Recognize and learn the differences and similarities between the two *kana* in each pair.

	o		*u*		*ra*
え	を	え	う	え	ら
ん	え	ネ	え	そ	え
n		(*ne*)		*so*	

✏️ Trace over the model *kana* below carefully. Try to maintain the correct overall shape of the *kana*.

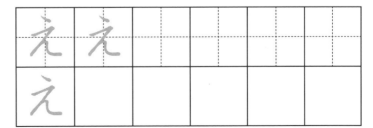

17

Hiragana

あいうえお　かきくけこ　さしすせそ　たちつてと　なにぬねの　はひふへほ　まみむめも　やゆよ　らりるれろ　わを　ん

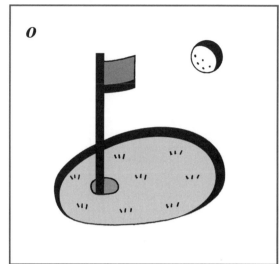

O is **o**ver the putting green flag, a golf ball flies.

💡 Look at the various forms of this *kana*. Notice what is and is not permissible as variants of the same *kana*.

🔍 Recognize and learn the differences and similarities between the two *kana* in each pair.

	mu		*ka*		*no*
お	む	お	か	お	の
あ	お	め	お	わ	お
a		*me*		*wa*	

✏️ Trace over the model *kana* below carefully. Try to maintain the correct overall shape of the *kana*.

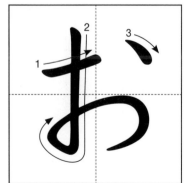

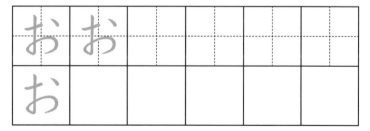

18

あいうえお **かきくけこ** さしすせそ たちつてと なにぬねの はひふへほ まみむめも やゆよ らりるれろ わを ん

Ka is the "**Kahh**!" of a crow behind a bent old woman.

💡 Look at the various forms of this *kana*. Notice what is and is not permissible as variants of the same *kana*.

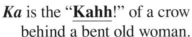

🔍 Recognize and learn the differences and similarities between the two *kana* in each pair.

                ke   *u*   *wa*

(*ka*)   (*ke*)   *ya*

✏️ Trace over the model *kana* below carefully. Try to maintain the correct overall shape of the *kana*.

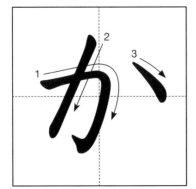

あいうえお **かきくけこ** さしすせそ たちつてと なにぬねの はひふへほ まみむめも やゆよ らりるれろ わを ん

Hiragana

Ki is a **key**.

💡 Look at the various forms of this *kana*. Notice what is and is not permissible as variants of the same *kana*.

🔍 Recognize and learn the differences and similarities between the two *kana* in each pair.

	mo		(*ki*)		(*yo*)

sa		*ma*		(*sa*)	

✏️ Trace over the model *kana* below carefully. Try to maintain the correct overall shape of the *kana*.

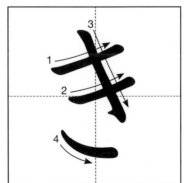

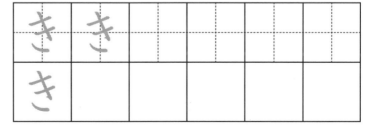

あいうえお **かきくけこ** さしすせそ たちつてと なにぬねの はひふへほ まみむめも やゆよ らりるれろ わを ん

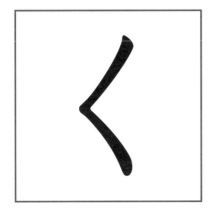

Ku is a cu**ck**oo's bill.

💡 Look at the various forms of this *kana*. Notice what is and is not permissible as variants of the same *kana*.

🔍 Recognize and learn the differences and similarities between the two *kana* in each pair.

	te		*(fu)*		*n*
く	て	く	フ	く	ん
へ	く	し	く	レ	く
he		*shi*		*(re)*	

✏️ Trace over the model *kana* below carefully. Try to maintain the correct overall shape of the *kana*.

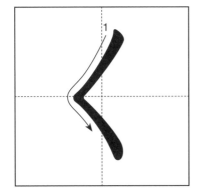

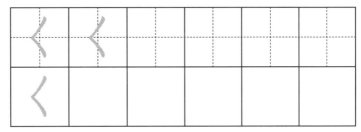

21

あいうえお **かきくけこ** さしすせそ たちつてと なにぬねの はひふへほ まみむめも やゆよ らりるれろ わを ん

Hiragana

Ke is one boxer being **K**O'd by another.

💡 Look at the various forms of this *kana*. Notice what is and is not permissible as variants of the same *kana*.

    け け

🔍 Recognize and learn the differences and similarities between the two *kana* in each pair.

	ni		*ri*		*ho*
け	に	け	り	け	ほ
は	け	た	け	い	け
ha		*ta*		*i*	

✏️ Trace over the model *kana* below carefully. Try to maintain the correct overall shape of the *kana*.

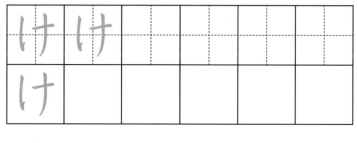

あいうえお **かきくけこ** さしすせそ たちつてと なにぬねの はひふへほ まみむめも やゆよ らりるれろ わを ん

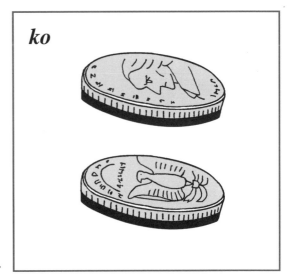

Ko is a stack of **co**ins.

💡 Look at the various forms of this *kana*. Notice what is and is not permissible as variants of the same *kana*.

🔍 Recognize and learn the differences and similarities between the two *kana* in each pair.

                          ni   *ri*   (*ko*)

i   (*ni*)   *sa*

✏️ Trace over the model *kana* below carefully. Try to maintain the correct overall shape of the *kana*.

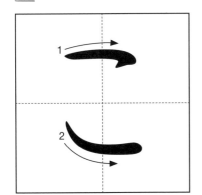 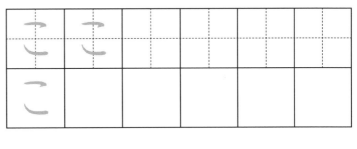

あいうえお かきくけこ **さしすせそ** たちつてと なにぬねの はひふへほ まみむめも やゆよ らりるれろ わを ん

Hiragana

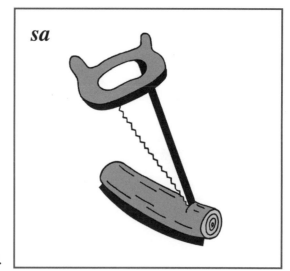

Sa is for **saw**ing a log.

💡 Look at the various forms of this *kana*. Notice what is and is not permissible as variants of the same *kana*.

🔍 Recognize and learn the differences and similarities between the two *kana* in each pair.

	chi		*(chi)*		*o*
さ	ち	さ	チ	さ	を
き	さ	け	さ	な	さ
ki		*ke*		*na*	

✏️ Trace over the model *kana* below carefully. Try to maintain the correct overall shape of the *kana*.

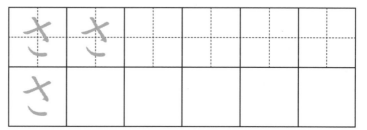

あいうえお　かきくけこ　**さしすせそ**　たちつてと　なにぬねの　はひふへほ　まみむめも　やゆよ　らりるれろ　わをん

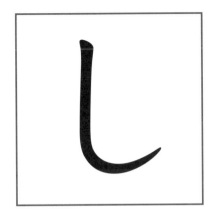

Shi is for "**She** has a ponytail."

💡 Look at the various forms of this *kana*. Notice what is and is not permissible as variants of the same *kana*.

🔍 Recognize and learn the differences and similarities between the two *kana* in each pair.

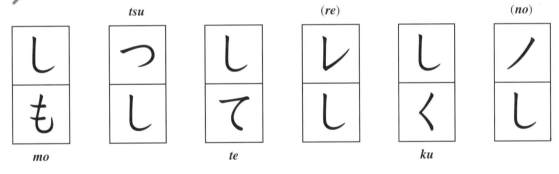

✏️ Trace over the model *kana* below carefully. Try to maintain the correct overall shape of the *kana*.

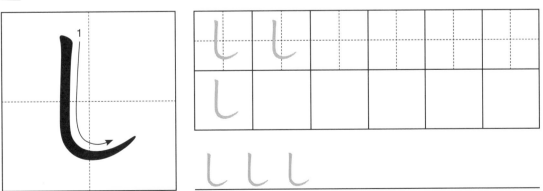

あいうえお かきくけこ **さしすせそ** たちつてと なにぬねの はひふへほ まみむめも やゆよ らりるれろ わを ん

Hiragana

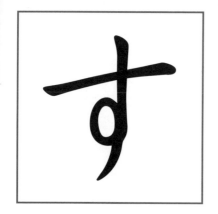

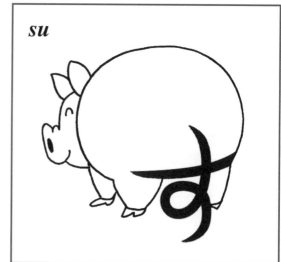

Su is "**Soo**ey, **soo**ey!" you call out to a pig with a curly tail.

💡 Look at the various forms of this *kana*. Notice what is and is not permissible as variants of the same *kana*.

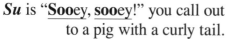

🔍 Recognize and learn the differences and similarities between the two *kana* in each pair.

o

mu

ha

yo

ma

(na)

✏️ Trace over the model *kana* below carefully. Try to maintain the correct overall shape of the *kana*.

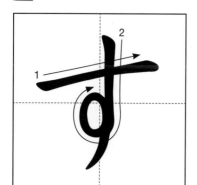

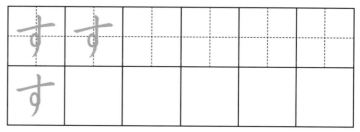

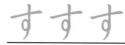

あいうえお　かきくけこ　**さしすせそ**　たちつてと　なにぬねの　はひふへほ　まみむめも　やゆよ　らりるれろ　わをん

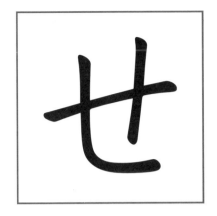

Se is to **say** "I love you!" on your boyfriend's lap.

💡 Look at the various forms of this *kana*. Notice what is and is not permissible as variants of the same *kana*.

🔍 Recognize and learn the differences and similarities between the two *kana* in each pair.

　　　　　　　　mi　　　　　　　　*(ya)*　　　　　　　　*ke*

  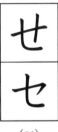

ya　　　　　　　*(se)*　　　　　　　*(sa)*

✏️ Trace over the model *kana* below carefully. Try to maintain the correct overall shape of the *kana*.

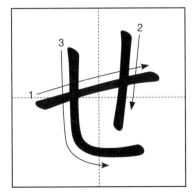 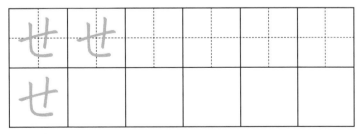

あいうえお かきくけこ **さしすせそ** たちつてと なにぬねの はひふへほ まみむめも やゆよ らりるれろ わを ん

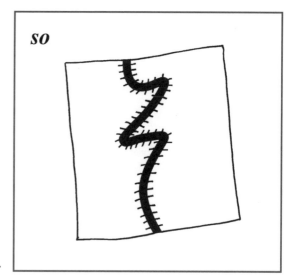

So is a zigzag **sew**ing stitch.

💡 Look at the various forms of this *kana*. Notice what is and is not permissible as variants of the same *kana*.

🔍 Recognize and learn the differences and similarities between the two *kana* in each pair.

        te   (*so*)   *e*

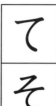

ro   *ru*   (*ne*)

✏️ Trace over the model *kana* below carefully. Try to maintain the correct overall shape of the *kana*.

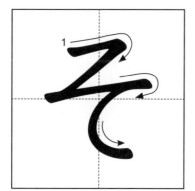
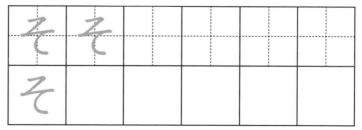

あいうえお　かきくけこ　さしすせそ　**たちつてと**　なにぬねの　はひふへほ　まみむめも　やゆよ　らりるれろ　わを　ん

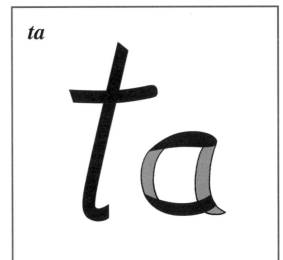

Ta is like the letters "**ta**."

💡 Look at the various forms of this *kana*. Notice what is and is not permissible as variants of the same *kana*.

た　た　た　た　た　た　た

 Recognize and learn the differences and similarities between the two *kana* in each pair.

	ha		ke		o
た	は	た	け	た	お
に	た	な	た	ほ	た
ni		na		ho	

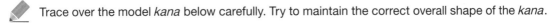 Trace over the model *kana* below carefully. Try to maintain the correct overall shape of the *kana*.

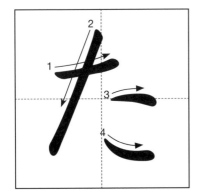

たた
た
たたた

あいうえお　かきくけこ　さしすせそ　**たちつてと**　なにぬねの　はひふへほ　まみむめも　やゆよ　らりるれろ　わを　ん

Hiragana

Chi is a **chee**rleader.

💡 Look at the various forms of this *kana*. Notice what is and is not permissible as variants of the same *kana*.

ち　ち　ち　ち　ち　ち　ち

🔍 Recognize and learn the differences and similarities between the two *kana* in each pair.

	tsu		*(ra)*		*sa*
ち	つ	ち	ラ	ち	さ
ら	ち	う	ち	ろ	ち
ra		*u*		*ro*	

✏️ Trace over the model *kana* below carefully. Try to maintain the correct overall shape of the *kana*.

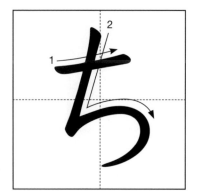

ち　ち

ち　ち

ち　ち　ち

30

あいうえお かきくけこ さしすせそ **たちつてと** なにぬねの はひふへほ まみむめも やゆよ らりるれろ わを ん

Tsu is a **tsu**nami, a huge sea wave.

💡 Look at the various forms of this *kana*. Notice what is and is not permissible as variants of the same *kana*.

🔍 Recognize and learn the differences and similarities between the two *kana* in each pair.

	te	*he*	*ra*

shi	*to*	*u*	

✏️ Trace over the model *kana* below carefully. Try to maintain the correct overall shape of the *kana*.

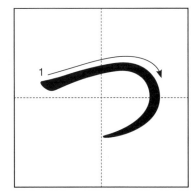
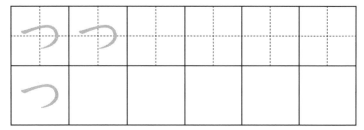

あいうえお かきくけこ さしすせそ **たちつてと** なにぬねの はひふへほ まみむめも やゆよ らりるれろ わを ん

Hiragana

Te is the **tai**l of a dog.

💡 Look at the various forms of this *kana*. Notice what is and is not permissible as variants of the same *kana*.

🔍 Recognize and learn the differences and similarities between the two *kana* in each pair.

| | **ku** | | **n** | | **(fu)** |

て　く　て　ん　て　フ
と　て　つ　て　し　て

to　　　　tsu　　　　shi

✏️ Trace over the model *kana* below carefully. Try to maintain the correct overall shape of the *kana*.

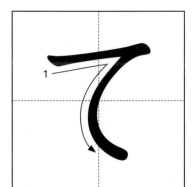
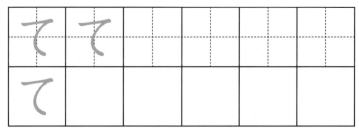

32

あいうえお かきくけこ さしすせそ **たちつてと** なにぬねの はひふへほ まみむめも やゆよ らりるれろ わを ん

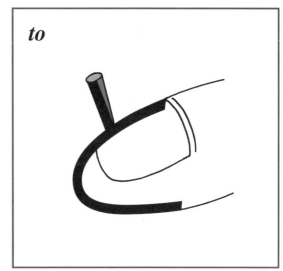

To is a <u>toe</u> with a thorn stuck in it.

💡 Look at the various forms of this *kana*. Notice what is and is not permissible as variants of the same *kana*.

🔍 Recognize and learn the differences and similarities between the two *kana* in each pair.

	ku		*sa*		(*ma*)
と	く	と	さ	と	マ
つ	と	ち	と	ヒ	と
tsu		*chi*		(*hi*)	

✏️ Trace over the model *kana* below carefully. Try to maintain the correct overall shape of the *kana*.

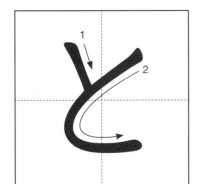

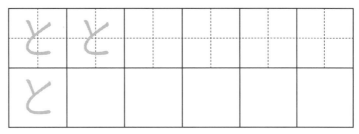

Hiragana

あいうえお　かきくけこ　さしすせそ　たちつてと　**なにぬねの**　はひふへほ　まみむめも　やゆよ　らりるれろ　わを　ん

Na is someone **kno**cking at the door.

💡 Look at the various forms of this *kana*. Notice what is and is not permissible as variants of the same *kana*.

🔍 Recognize and learn the differences and similarities between the two *kana* in each pair.

な	ta た	な	ho ほ	な	mu む
は	な	に	な	け	な
ha		ni		ke	

✏️ Trace over the model *kana* below carefully. Try to maintain the correct overall shape of the *kana*.

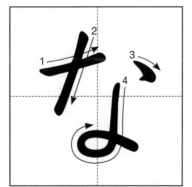
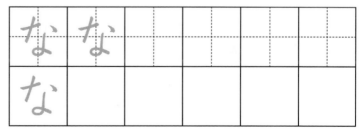

あいうえお　かきくけこ　さしすせそ　たちつてと　**なにぬねの**　はひふへほ　まみむめも　やゆよ　らりるれろ　わを　ん

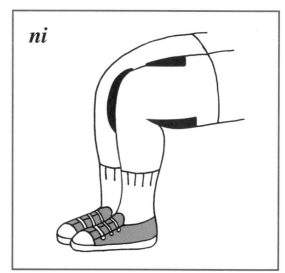

Ni is a **knee**.

💡 Look at the various forms of this *kana*. Notice what is and is not permissible as variants of the same *kana*.

🔍 Recognize and learn the differences and similarities between the two *kana* in each pair.

	ke		*i*		*(ko)*
	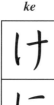			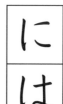	
ko	*ta*		*ha*		

✏️ Trace over the model *kana* below carefully. Try to maintain the correct overall shape of the *kana*.

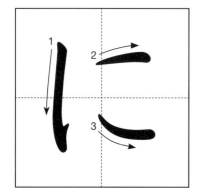

35

Hiragana

あいうえお かきくけこ さしすせそ たちつてと **なにぬねの** はひふへほ まみむめも やゆよ らりるれろ わを ん

Nu is a **new** trike.

💡 Look at the various forms of this *kana*. Notice what is and is not permissible as variants of the same *kana*.

🔍 Recognize and learn the differences and similarities between the two *kana* in each pair.

	ne		a		o
me		no		yu	

✏️ Trace over the model *kana* below carefully. Try to maintain the correct overall shape of the *kana*.

あいうえお かきくけこ さしすせそ たちつてと **なにぬねの** はひふへほ まみむめも やゆよ らりるれろ わを ん

Ne is a s**nai**l behind a **nai**l.

💡 Look at the various forms of this *kana*. Notice what is and is not permissible as variants of the same *kana*.

🔍 Recognize and learn the differences and similarities between the two *kana* in each pair.

	wa		*me*		*yu*
ね	わ	ね	め	ね	ゆ
ぬ	ね	れ	ね	る	ね
nu	*re*			*ru*	

✏️ Trace over the model *kana* below carefully. Try to maintain the correct overall shape of the *kana*.

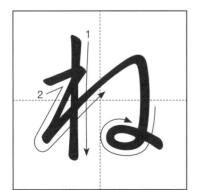
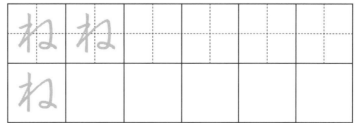

Hiragana

あいうえお かきくけこ さしすせそ たちつてと **なにぬねの** はひふへほ まみむめも やゆよ らりるれろ わを ん

No is a **no** entry sign.

💡 Look at the various forms of this *kana*. Notice what is and is not permissible as variants of the same *kana*.

🔍 Recognize and learn the differences and similarities between the two *kana* in each pair.

	me		*yu*		*o*
tsu	*a*		*nu*		

✏️ Trace over the model *kana* below carefully. Try to maintain the correct overall shape of the *kana*.

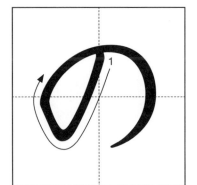 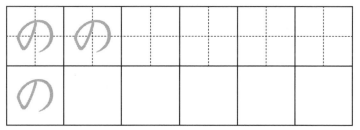

38

あいうえお　かきくけこ　さしすせそ　たちつてと　なにぬねの　**はひふへほ**　まみむめも　やゆよ　らりるれろ　わを　ん

Ha is a **ho**ckey player sitting on a bench.

💡 Look at the various forms of this *kana*. Notice what is and is not permissible as variants of the same *kana*.

| は | は | は | は | は | は | は |

🔍 Recognize and learn the differences and similarities between the two *kana* in each pair.

	ni		*ke*		*ta*
は	に	は	け	は	た
ほ	は	ま	は	な	は
ho		*ma*		*na*	

✏️ Trace over the model *kana* below carefully. Try to maintain the correct overall shape of the *kana*.

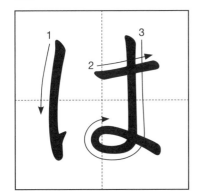

ははは

は

ははは

39

あいうえお　かきくけこ　さしすせそ　たちつてと　なにぬねの　**はひふへほ**　まみむめも　やゆよ　らりるれろ　わを　ん

Hiragana

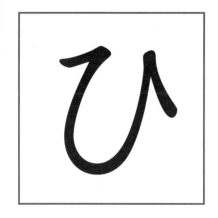

Hi is to laugh "**Hee**-**hee**!"

💡 Look at the various forms of this *kana*. Notice what is and is not permissible as variants of the same *kana*.

🔍 Recognize and learn the differences and similarities between the two *kana* in each pair.

shi		to		ra
ひ / て	し / ひ	ひ / つ	と / ひ	ひ / も	ら / ひ
te		tsu		mo	

✏️ Trace over the model *kana* below carefully. Try to maintain the correct overall shape of the *kana*.

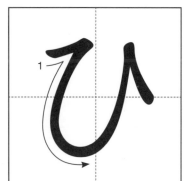
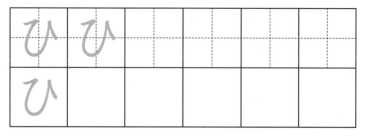

あいうえお かきくけこ さしすせそ たちつてと なにぬねの **はひふへほ** まみむめも やゆよ らりるれろ わを ん

fu/hu

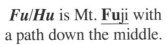

Fu/Hu is Mt. **Fu**ji with a path down the middle.

💡 Look at the various forms of this *kana*. Notice what is and is not permissible as variants of the same *kana*.

🔍 Recognize and learn the differences and similarities between the two *kana* in each pair.

	na		(*ha*)		*ya*
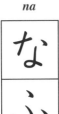					
(*ho*)		*u*		*ro*	

✏️ Trace over the model *kana* below carefully. Try to maintain the correct overall shape of the *kana*.

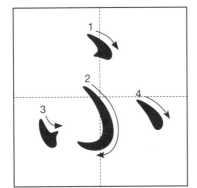

あいうえお かきくけこ さしすせそ たちつてと なにぬねの **はひふへほ** まみむめも やゆよ らりるれろ わを ん

Hiragana

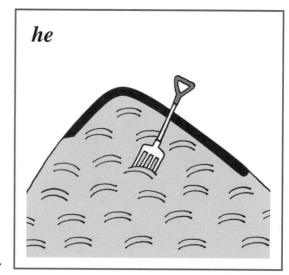

He is a **hay**stack.

💡 Look at the various forms of this *kana*. Notice what is and is not permissible as variants of the same *kana*.

🔍 Recognize and learn the differences and similarities between the two *kana* in each pair.

	shi		*te*		*(re)*
へ	し	へ	て	へ	レ
く	へ	つ	へ	フ	へ
ku		*tsu*		*(fu)*	

✏️ Trace over the model *kana* below carefully. Try to maintain the correct overall shape of the *kana*.

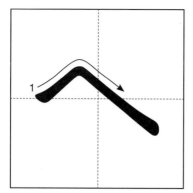
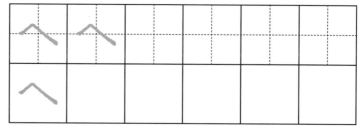

あいうえお　かきくけこ　さしすせそ　たちつてと　なにぬねの　**はひふへほ**　まみむめも　やゆよ　らりるれろ　わを　ん

Ho is a **hoe** held by a farmer with a big hat, sitting with his legs crossed.

💡 Look at the various forms of this *kana*. Notice what is and is not permissible as variants of the same *kana*.

🔍 Recognize and learn the differences and similarities between the two *kana* in each pair.

	ke		*ni*		*ki*
ほ	け	ほ	に	ほ	き
は	ほ	ま	ほ	な	ほ
ha		*ma*		*na*	

✏️ Trace over the model *kana* below carefully. Try to maintain the correct overall shape of the *kana*.

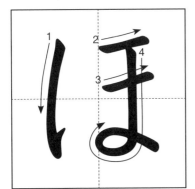

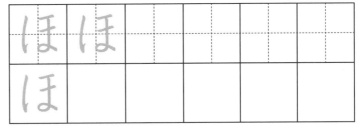

43

Hiragana

あいうえお かきくけこ さしすせそ たちつてと なにぬねの はひふへほ **まみむめも** やゆよ らりるれろ わを ん

Ma is Grand**ma** with a hat.

💡 Look at the various forms of this *kana*. Notice what is and is not permissible as variants of the same *kana*.

🔍 Recognize and learn the differences and similarities between the two *kana* in each pair.

ま	ha	ま	su	ま	o
ほ	は	も	す	き	お
ho	ま	mo	ま	ki	ま

✏️ Trace over the model *kana* below carefully. Try to maintain the correct overall shape of the *kana*.

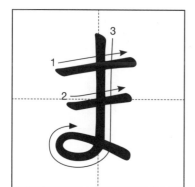

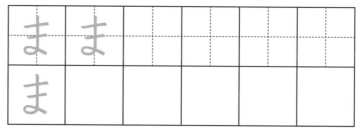

あいうえお　かきくけこ　さしすせそ　たちつてと　なにぬねの　はひふへほ　**まみむめも**　やゆよ　らりるれろ　わを　ん

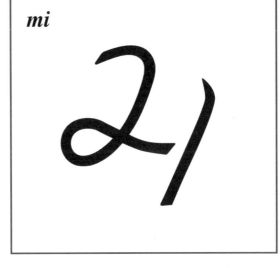

Mi is <u>me</u>, 21 years old, a nice age to be.

💡 Look at the various forms of this *kana*. Notice what is and is not permissible as variants of the same *kana*.

🔍 Recognize and learn the differences and similarities between the two *kana* in each pair.

	se		*ro*		*ma*
		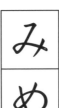			
ya	*me*		*mu*		

✏️ Trace over the model *kana* below carefully. Try to maintain the correct overall shape of the *kana*.

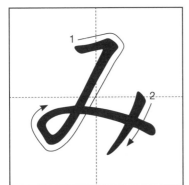

45

Hiragana

あいうえお　かきくけこ　さしすせそ　たちつてと　なにぬねの　はひふへほ　**まみむめも**　やゆよ　らりるれろ　わを　ん

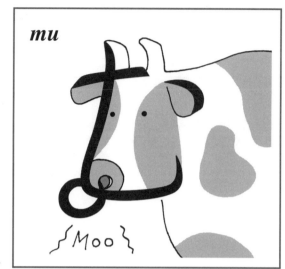

Mu is the **moo**ing face of a cow.

💡 Look at the various forms of this *kana*. Notice what is and is not permissible as variants of the same *kana*.

🔍 Recognize and learn the differences and similarities between the two *kana* in each pair.

	o		mi		ka
む	お	む	み	む	か
す	む	ち	む	な	む
su		chi		na	

✏️ Trace over the model *kana* below carefully. Try to maintain the correct overall shape of the *kana*.

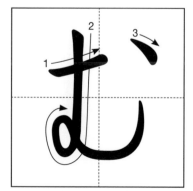
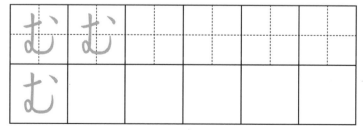

46

あいうえお　かきくけこ　さしすせそ　たちつてと　なにぬねの　はひふへほ　**まみむめも**　やゆよ　らりるれろ　わを　ん

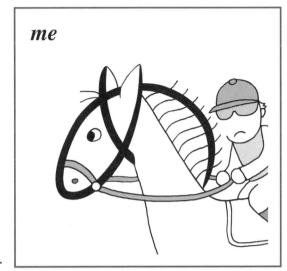

me

Me is the **ma**ne of a horse.

💡 Look at the various forms of this *kana*. Notice what is and is not permissible as variants of the same *kana*.

🔍 Recognize and learn the differences and similarities between the two *kana* in each pair.

	wa		*no*		*mi*
nu		*ne*		*a*	

✏️ Trace over the model *kana* below carefully. Try to maintain the correct overall shape of the *kana*.

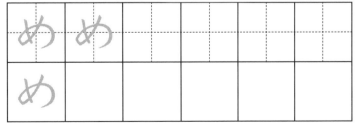

Hiragana

あいうえお かきくけこ さしすせそ たちつてと なにぬねの はひふへほ **まみむめも** やゆよ らりるれろ わを ん

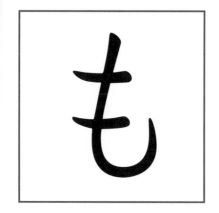

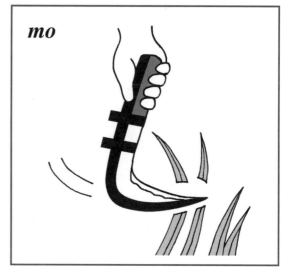

mo

Mo is for **mow**ing grass with a sickle.

💡 Look at the various forms of this *kana*. Notice what is and is not permissible as variants of the same *kana*.

🔍 Recognize and learn the differences and similarities between the two *kana* in each pair.

shi		(*ki*)		*tsu*
も	し	も	キ	も
ま	も	き	モ	つ
				も
ma		*ki*	(*mo*)	

✏️ Trace over the model *kana* below carefully. Try to maintain the correct overall shape of the *kana*.

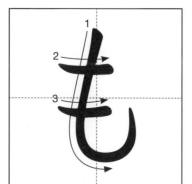

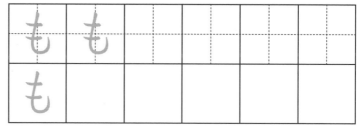

あいうえお　かきくけこ　さしすせそ　たちつてと　なにぬねの　はひふへほ　まみむめも　**やゆよ**　らりるれろ　わを　ん

ya

Ya is the "**Ya**!" Germans say when drinking beer from a big mug.

💡 Look at the various forms of this *kana*. Notice what is and is not permissible as variants of the same *kana*.

🔍 Recognize and learn the differences and similarities between the two *kana* in each pair.

	mi		(*se*)		(*ya*)

se		*tsu*		(*sa*)	

✏️ Trace over the model *kana* below carefully. Try to maintain the correct overall shape of the *kana*.

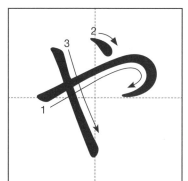

49

Hiragana

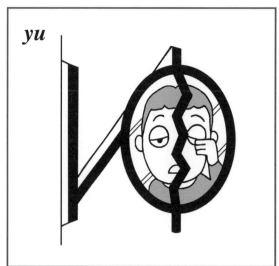

Yu is sleepy **you** in the morning when your mirror cracks.

💡 Look at the various forms of this *kana*. Notice what is and is not permissible as variants of the same *kana*.

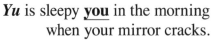

🔍 Recognize and learn the differences and similarities between the two *kana* in each pair.

	ya		ru		no
ゆ	や	ゆ	る	ゆ	の
わ	ゆ	あ	ゆ	め	ゆ
wa		a		me	

✏️ Trace over the model *kana* below carefully. Try to maintain the correct overall shape of the *kana*.

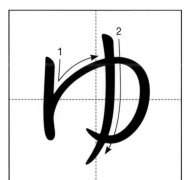
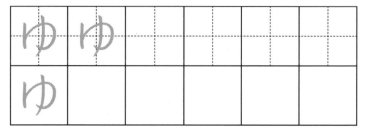

あいうえお　かきくけこ　さしすせそ　たちつてと　なにぬねの　はひふへほ　まみむめも　**やゆよ**　らりるれろ　わを　ん

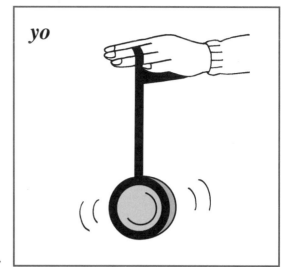

Yo is a **yo**-**yo**.

💡 Look at the various forms of this *kana*. Notice what is and is not permissible as variants of the same *kana*.

🔍 Recognize and learn the differences and similarities between the two *kana* in each pair.

	o		*ho*		*mu*
	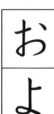			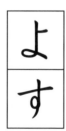	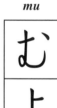
ha	*ma*		*su*		

✏️ Trace over the model *kana* below carefully. Try to maintain the correct overall shape of the *kana*.

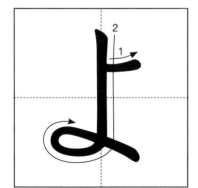
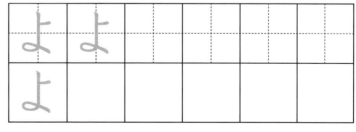

あいうえお かきくけこ さしすせそ たちつてと なにぬねの はひふへほ まみむめも やゆよ **らりるれろ** わを ん

Hiragana

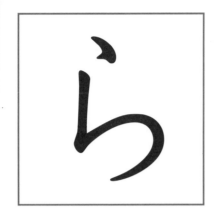

Ra is the "**Rah**!" you shout through a megaphone at a game.

💡 Look at the various forms of this *kana*. Notice what is and is not permissible as variants of the same *kana*.

🔍 Recognize and learn the differences and similarities between the two *kana* in each pair.

 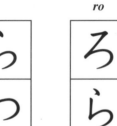  

chi   tsu   o

✏️ Trace over the model *kana* below carefully. Try to maintain the correct overall shape of the *kana*.

52

あいうえお　かきくけこ　さしすせそ　たちつてと　なにぬねの　はひふへほ　まみむめも　やゆよ　**らりるれろ**　わを　ん

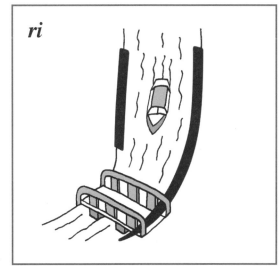

Ri is a **ri**ver.

💡 Look at the various forms of this *kana*. Notice what is and is not permissible as variants of the same *kana*.

🔍 Recognize and learn the differences and similarities between the two *kana* in each pair.

	ko		*(ru)*		*(ha)*
り	こ	り	ル	り	ハ
い	り	ニ	り	ソ	り
i		*(ni)*		*(so)*	

✏️ Trace over the model *kana* below carefully. Try to maintain the correct overall shape of the *kana*.

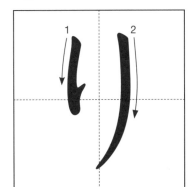
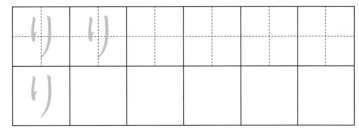

あいうえお　かきくけこ　さしすせそ　たちつてと　なにぬねの　はひふへほ　まみむめも　やゆよ　**ら**り**る**れ**ろ**　わを　ん

Hiragana

Ru is a lasso **loo**p.

💡 Look at the various forms of this *kana*. Notice what is and is not permissible as variants of the same *kana*.

🔍 Recognize and learn the differences and similarities between the two *kana* in each pair.

	chi		*nu*		*su*
る	ち	る	ぬ	る	す
ろ	る	ら	る	ね	る
ro		*ra*		*ne*	

✏️ Trace over the model *kana* below carefully. Try to maintain the correct overall shape of the *kana*.

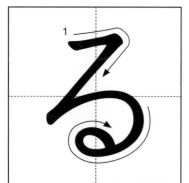
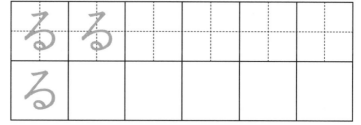

54

あいうえお かきくけこ さしすせそ たちつてと なにぬねの はひふへほ まみむめも やゆよ **らりるれろ** わを ん

Re is a **ra**dio tower catching **ra**dio waves.

💡 Look at the various forms of this *kana*. Notice what is and is not permissible as variants of the same *kana*.

🔍 Recognize and learn the differences and similarities between the two *kana* in each pair.

     ne   *n*   *yu*

wa   *me*   *so*

✏️ Trace over the model *kana* below carefully. Try to maintain the correct overall shape of the *kana*.

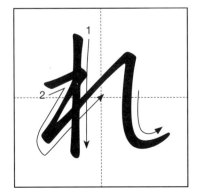

55

Hiragana

あいうえお かきくけこ さしすせそ たちつてと なにぬねの はひふへほ まみむめも やゆよ **らりるれろ** わを ん

Ro is a twisted **ro**pe.

💡 Look at the various forms of this *kana*. Notice what is and is not permissible as variants of the same *kana*.

ろ ろ ろ ろ ろ ろ ろ

🔍 Recognize and learn the differences and similarities between the two *kana* in each pair.

	ra		*so*		*chi*
ろ	ら	ろ	そ	ろ	ち
る	ろ	う	ろ	わ	ろ
ru		*u*		*wa*	

✏️ Trace over the model *kana* below carefully. Try to maintain the correct overall shape of the *kana*.

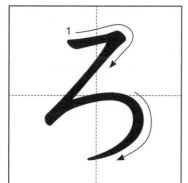

ろ ろ

ろ ろ

ろ ろ ろ

あいうえお かきくけこ さしすせそ たちつてと なにぬねの はひふへほ まみむめも やゆよ らりるれろ **わ**を ん

Wa is a **swa**n behind a stake.

💡 Look at the various forms of this *kana*. Notice what is and is not permissible as variants of the same *kana*.

🔍 Recognize and learn the differences and similarities between the two *kana* in each pair.

	ne		*ra*		*tsu*
わ	ね	わ	ら	わ	つ
れ	わ	ゆ	わ	ろ	わ
re		*yu*		*ro*	

✏️ Trace over the model *kana* below carefully. Try to maintain the correct overall shape of the *kana*.

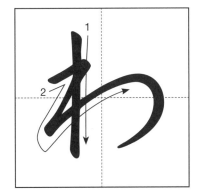

57

Hiragana

あいうえお　かきくけこ　さしすせそ　たちつてと　なにぬねの　はひふへほ　まみむめも　やゆよ　らりるれろ　**わを**　ん

O is an **o**ld skater skillfully skating.

💡 Look at the various forms of this *kana*. Notice what is and is not permissible as variants of the same *kana*.

🔍 Recognize and learn the differences and similarities between the two *kana* in each pair.

	chi		*so*		*o*
を	ち	を	そ	を	お
と	を	え	を	ネ	を
to		*e*		*(ne)*	

✏️ Trace over the model *kana* below carefully. Try to maintain the correct overall shape of the *kana*.

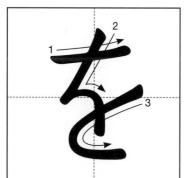
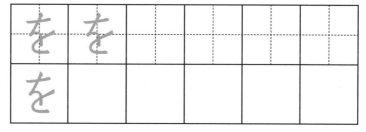

あいうえお　かきくけこ　さしすせそ　たちつてと　なにぬねの　はひふへほ　まみむめも　やゆよ　らりるれろ　わを　ん

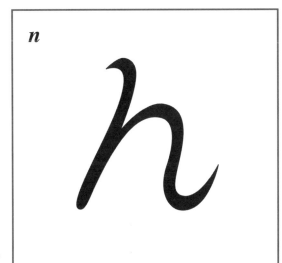

N is a small cursive "n (e**n**)."

💡 Look at the various forms of this *kana*. Notice what is and is not permissible as variants of the same *kana*.

🔍 Recognize and learn the differences and similarities between the two *kana* in each pair.

	shi		*e*		*re*
ん	し	ん	え	ん	れ
く	ん	レ	へ	ん	ん
ku		(*re*)		*he*	

✏️ Trace over the model *kana* below carefully. Try to maintain the correct overall shape of the *kana*.

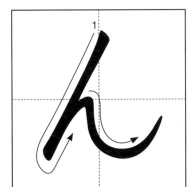
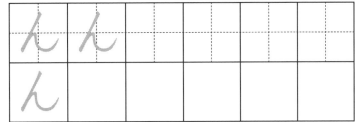

59

Katakana

Just like *hiragana*, there are 46 basic *katakana* characters. Modified *katakana* characters based on these basic ones represent the remaining syllables. For the explanations of such modifications, see the end of this book.

	a	i	u	e	o
	ア	イ	ウ	エ	オ
k-	カ	キ	ク	ケ	コ
s-	サ	シ	ス	セ	ソ
t-	タ	チ	ツ	テ	ト
n-	ナ	ニ	ヌ	ネ	ノ
h-	ハ	ヒ	フ	ヘ	ホ
m-	マ	ミ	ム	メ	モ
y-	ヤ		ユ		ヨ
r-	ラ	リ	ル	レ	ロ
w-	ワ				ヲ
n	ン				

アイウエオ カキクケコ サシスセソ タチツテト ナニヌネノ ハヒフヘホ マミムメモ ヤユヨ ラリルレロ ワヲ ン

Katakana

A is a "**Ahh**!" a hippo shouts.

💡 Look at the various forms of this *kana*. Notice what is and is not permissible as variants of the same *kana*.

🔍 Recognize and learn the differences and similarities between the two *kana* in each pair.

	te		*wa*		*ya*
ア	テ	ア	ワ	ア	ヤ
マ	ア	フ	ア	ム	ア
ma		*fu*		*mu*	

✏️ Trace over the model *kana* below carefully. Try to maintain the correct overall shape of the *kana*.

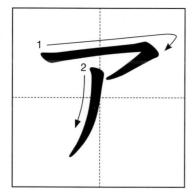

62

アイウエオ　カキクケコ　サシスセソ　タチツテト　ナニヌネノ　ハヒフヘホ　マミムメモ　ヤユヨ　ラリルレロ　ワヲ　ン

I is an **ea**sel holding a picture.

💡 Look at the various forms of this *kana*. Notice what is and is not permissible as variants of the same *kana*.

🔍 Recognize and learn the differences and similarities between the two *kana* in each pair.

su		me		na
イ	イ	メ	イ	ナ
ト	イ	ノ	リ	イ
to	no		ri	

✏️ Trace over the model *kana* below carefully. Try to maintain the correct overall shape of the *kana*.

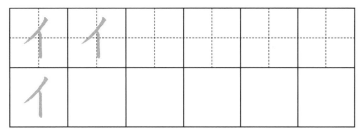

63

アイウエオ カキクケコ サシスセソ タチツテト ナニヌネノ ハヒフヘホ マミムメモ ヤユヨ ラリルレロ ワヲ ン

Katakana

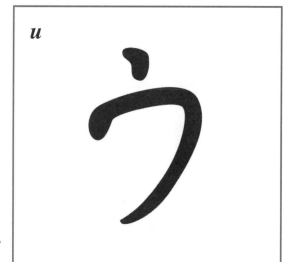
u

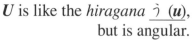
U is like the *hiragana* う (*u*), but is angular.

💡 Look at the various forms of this *kana*. Notice what is and is not permissible as variants of the same *kana*.

🔍 Recognize and learn the differences and similarities between the two *kana* in each pair.

	ra		(*ro*)		(*u*)
ウ	ラ	ウ	ろ	ウ	う
ワ	ウ	ヲ	ウ	フ	ウ
wa		*o*		*fu*	

✏️ Trace over the model *kana* below carefully. Try to maintain the correct overall shape of the *kana*.

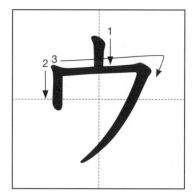

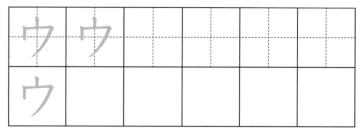

アイ**エ**オ　カキクケコ　サシスセソ　タチツテト　ナニヌネノ　ハヒフヘホ　マミムメモ　ヤユヨ　ラリルレロ　ワヲ　ン

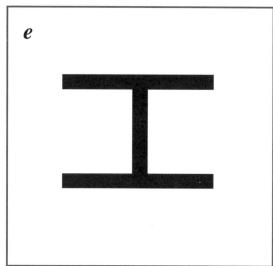

E is a capital "H (**ai**ch)" lying on its side.

💡 Look at the various forms of this *kana*. Notice what is and is not permissible as variants of the same *kana*.

🔍 Recognize and learn the differences and similarities between the two *kana* in each pair.

	ni		*ki*		*mi*
エ	ニ	エ	キ	エ	ミ
コ	エ	ユ	エ	こ	エ
ko		*yu*		(*ko*)	

✏️ Trace over the model *kana* below carefully. Try to maintain the correct overall shape of the *kana*.

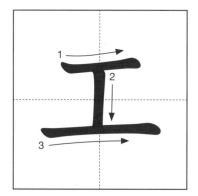

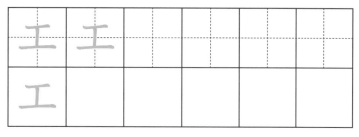

65

アイウ**エ**オ カキクケコ サシスセソ タチツテト ナニヌネノ ハヒフヘホ マミムメモ ヤユヨ ラリルレロ ワヲ ン

Katakana

O is for "**Oh**, what a good dancer!"

💡 Look at the various forms of this *kana*. Notice what is and is not permissible as variants of the same *kana*.

🔍 Recognize and learn the differences and similarities between the two *kana* in each pair.

	o			*i*		*ne*
オ	ヲ	オ	イ	オ	ネ
ナ	オ	ホ	オ	お	オ
na		*ho*		(*o*)	

✏️ Trace over the model *kana* below carefully. Try to maintain the correct overall shape of the *kana*.

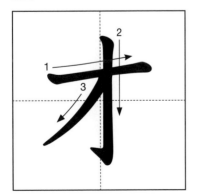

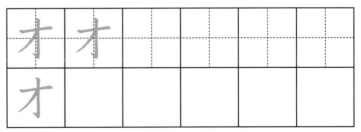

66

アイウエオ **カキクケコ** サシスセソ タチツテト ナニヌネノ ハヒフヘホ マミムメモ ヤユヨ ラリルレロ ワヲ ン

Ka is an angular *hiragana* か (**ka**) without the crow.

💡 Look at the various forms of this *kana*. Notice what is and is not permissible as variants of the same *kana*.

| カ | カ | **カ** | **カ** | カ | ђ | **カ** |

🔍 Recognize and learn the differences and similarities between the two *kana* in each pair.

	ma		*ku*		(*ka*)
カ	マ	カ	ク	カ	か
ア	カ	ヤ	カ	ワ	カ
a		*ya*		*wa*	

✏️ Trace over the model *kana* below carefully. Try to maintain the correct overall shape of the *kana*.

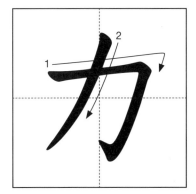

67

アイウエオ **カキクケコ** サシスセソ タチツテト ナニヌネノ ハヒフヘホ マミムメモ ヤユヨ ラリルレロ ワヲ ン

Katakana

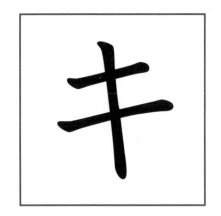

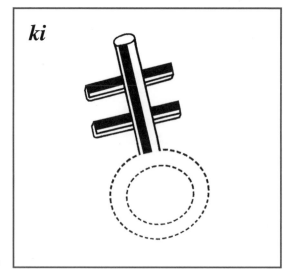

ki

Ki is a **key** without a loop.

💡 Look at the various forms of this *kana*. Notice what is and is not permissible as variants of the same *kana*.

🔍 Recognize and learn the differences and similarities between the two *kana* in each pair.

    chi   (*sa*)   (*ki*)

te   o   mo

 Trace over the model *kana* below carefully. Try to maintain the correct overall shape of the *kana*.

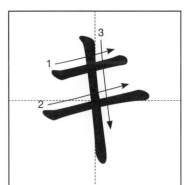

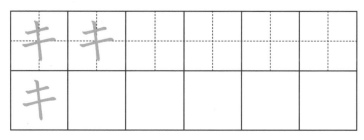

アイウエオ **カキクケコ** サシスセソ タチツテト ナニヌネノ ハヒフヘホ マミムメモ ヤユヨ ラリルレロ ワヲ ン

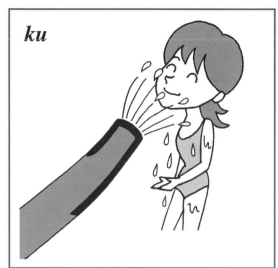
ku

Ku is to **coo**l yourself with **coo**l water from a hose.

💡 Look at the various forms of this *kana*. Notice what is and is not permissible as variants of the same *kana*.

🔍 Recognize and learn the differences and similarities between the two *kana* in each pair.

	fu		*o*		*ri*
ク	フ	ク	ヲ	ク	リ
ワ	ク	タ	ク	マ	ク
wa		*ta*		*ma*	

✏️ Trace over the model *kana* below carefully. Try to maintain the correct overall shape of the *kana*.

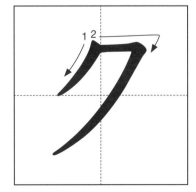

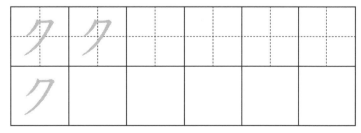

アイウエオ **カキクケコ** サシスセソ タチツテト ナニヌネノ ハヒフヘホ マミムメモ ヤユヨ ラリルレロ ワヲ ン

Katakana

Ke is a lopsided "K (**kay**)."

💡 Look at the various forms of this *kana*. Notice what is and is not permissible as variants of the same *kana*.

 Recognize and learn the differences and similarities between the two *kana* in each pair.

	o		na		wa
ケ	オ	ケ	ナ	ケ	ワ
テ	ケ	チ	ケ	ク	ケ
te		chi		ku	

✏️ Trace over the model *kana* below carefully. Try to maintain the correct overall shape of the *kana*.

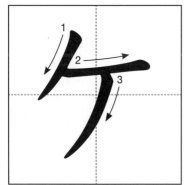

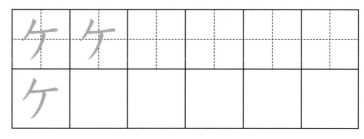

アイウエオ **カキクケコ** サシスセソ タチツテト ナニヌネノ ハヒフヘホ マミムメモ ヤユヨ ラリルレロ ワヲ ン

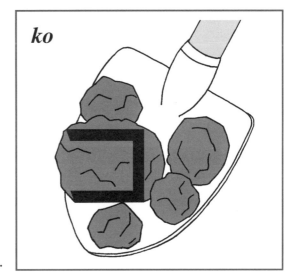

ko

Ko is a piece of **coa**l.

💡 Look at the various forms of this *kana*. Notice what is and is not permissible as variants of the same *kana*.

🔍 Recognize and learn the differences and similarities between the two *kana* in each pair.

	e			*ni*		*ro*
コ	エ	コ	ニ	コ	ロ
ユ	コ	こ	コ	ヨ	コ
yu		(*ko*)		*yo*	

 Trace over the model *kana* below carefully. Try to maintain the correct overall shape of the *kana*.

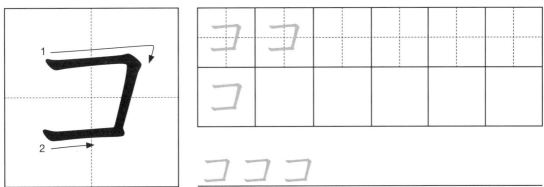

71

アイウエオ　カキクケコ　**サシスセソ**　タチツテト　ナニヌネノ　ハヒフヘホ　マミムメモ　ヤユヨ　ラリルレロ　ワヲ　ン

Katakana

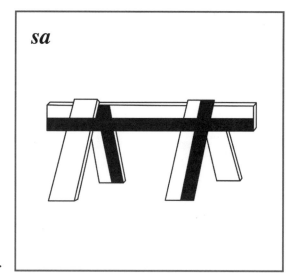

Sa is a **saw**horse.

💡 Look at the various forms of this *kana*. Notice what is and is not permissible as variants of the same *kana*.

サ	サ	サ	サ	サ	サ	サ

🔍 Recognize and learn the differences and similarities between the two *kana* in each pair.

	se		*wa*		*na*
サ	セ	サ	ワ	サ	ナ
セ	サ	ク	サ	フ	サ
(*se*)		*ku*		*fu*	

✏️ Trace over the model *kana* below carefully. Try to maintain the correct overall shape of the *kana*.

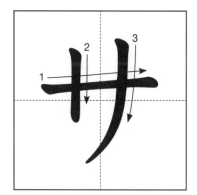

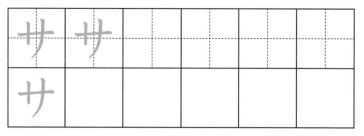

72

アイウエオ　カキクケコ　**サシスセソ**　タチツテト　ナニヌネノ　ハヒフヘホ　マミムメモ　ヤユヨ　ラリルレロ　ワヲ　ン

shi

Shi is for "**She** has good-looking lips and jaws."

💡 Look at the various forms of this *kana*. Notice what is and is not permissible as variants of the same *kana*.

🔍 Recognize and learn the differences and similarities between the two *kana* in each pair.

	mi		so		o

tsu	n			ni	

✏️ Trace over the model *kana* below carefully. Try to maintain the correct overall shape of the *kana*.

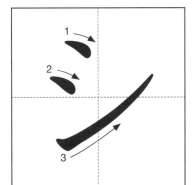

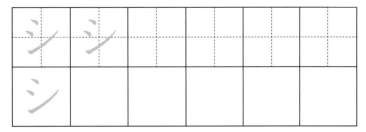

73

アイウエオ　カキクケコ　**サシスセソ**　タチツテト　ナニヌネノ　ハヒフヘホ　マミムメモ　ヤユヨ　ラリルレロ　ワヲ　ン

Katakana

su

Su is **Su**perman.

💡 Look at the various forms of this *kana*. Notice what is and is not permissible as variants of the same *kana*.

🔍 Recognize and learn the differences and similarities between the two *kana* in each pair.

	ma		*me*		*ta*
ス	マ	ス	メ	ス	タ
フ	ス	ヌ	ス	ケ	ス
fu		*nu*		*ke*	

✏️ Trace over the model *kana* below carefully. Try to maintain the correct overall shape of the *kana*.

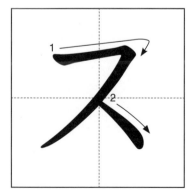
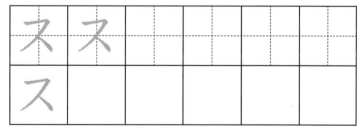

アイウエオ カキクケコ **サシスセソ** タチツテト ナニヌネノ ハヒフヘホ マミムメモ ヤユヨ ラリルレロ ワヲ ン

Se is to **say** "I love you too!"

💡 Look at the various forms of this *kana*. Notice what is and is not permissible as variants of the same *kana*.

| セ | セ | セ | セ | セ | セ | セ |

🔍 Recognize and learn the differences and similarities between the two *kana* in each pair.

	ma		*sa*		*(se)*
セ	マ	セ	サ	セ	せ
ヤ	セ	ヒ	セ	ア	セ
ya		*hi*		*a*	

 Trace over the model *kana* below carefully. Try to maintain the correct overall shape of the *kana*.

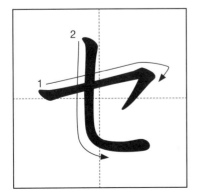

Katakana

アイウエオ　カキクケコ　**サシスセソ**　タチツテト　ナニヌネノ　ハヒフヘホ　マミムメモ　ヤユヨ　ラリルレロ　ワヲ　ン

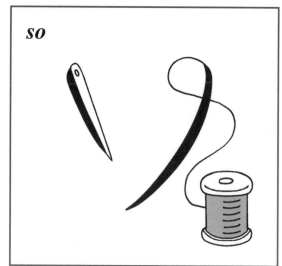

so

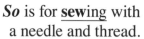

So is for **sew**ing with a needle and thread.

💡 Look at the various forms of this *kana*. Notice what is and is not permissible as variants of the same *kana*.

🔍 Recognize and learn the differences and similarities between the two *kana* in each pair.

	tsu		*ri*		(*i*)
		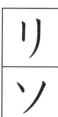			
n	*shi*		*ha*		

✏️ Trace over the model *kana* below carefully. Try to maintain the correct overall shape of the *kana*.

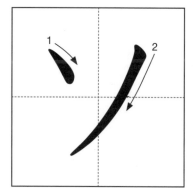
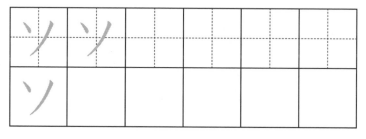

アイウエオ　カキクケコ　サシスセソ　**タチツテト**　ナニヌネノ　ハヒフヘホ　マミムメモ　ヤユヨ　ラリルレロ　ワヲ　ン

Ta is the Leaning **To**wer of Pisa.

💡 Look at the various forms of this *kana*. Notice what is and is not permissible as variants of the same *kana*.

🔍 Recognize and learn the differences and similarities between the two *kana* in each pair.

	wa		ma		me
タ	ワ	タ	マ	タ	メ
ク	タ	ヌ	タ	ヲ	タ
ku		nu		o	

✏️ Trace over the model *kana* below carefully. Try to maintain the correct overall shape of the *kana*.

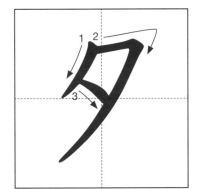

77

アイウエオ カキクケコ サシスセソ **タチツテト** ナニヌネノ ハヒフヘホ マミムメモ ヤユヨ ラリルレロ ワヲ ン

Katakana

Chi is a **chee**rleader.

💡 Look at the various forms of this *kana*. Notice what is and is not permissible as variants of the same *kana*.

🔍 Recognize and learn the differences and similarities between the two *kana* in each pair.

	te		*sa*		*ki*
チ	テ	チ	サ	チ	キ
ナ	チ	ヌ	チ	モ	チ
na		*nu*		*mo*	

 Trace over the model *kana* below carefully. Try to maintain the correct overall shape of the *kana*.

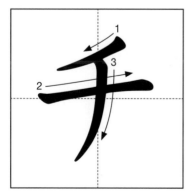

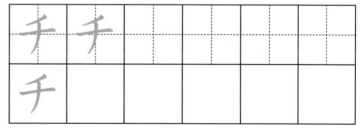

78

アイウエオ カキクケコ サシスセソ **タチツテト** ナニヌネノ ハヒフヘホ マミムメモ ヤユヨ ラリルレロ ワヲ ン

tsu

Tsu is a <u>cat's</u> whiskers.

💡 Look at the various forms of this *kana*. Notice what is and is not permissible as variants of the same *kana*.

🔍 Recognize and learn the differences and similarities between the two *kana* in each pair.

	so		*wa*		*ra*
ツ	ソ	ツ	ワ	ツ	ラ
シ	ツ	ン	ツ	ミ	ツ
shi		*n*		*mi*	

✏️ Trace over the model *kana* below carefully. Try to maintain the correct overall shape of the *kana*.

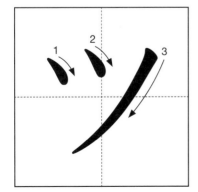

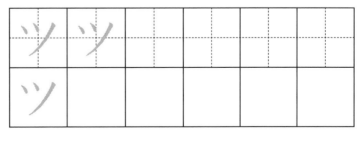

79

Katakana

アイウエオ カキクケコ サシスセソ **タチツテト** ナニヌネノ ハヒフヘホ マミムメモ ヤユヨ ラリルレロ ワヲ ン

Te is a **ta**ble.

💡 Look at the various forms of this *kana*. Notice what is and is not permissible as variants of the same *kana*.

テ	テ	テ	テ	テ	テ	テ

🔍 Recognize and learn the differences and similarities between the two *kana* in each pair.

	na		*ra*		*mo*
テ	ナ	テ	ラ	テ	モ
チ	テ	ヲ	テ	二	テ
chi		*o*		*ni*	

✏️ Trace over the model *kana* below carefully. Try to maintain the correct overall shape of the *kana*.

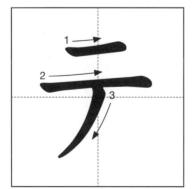

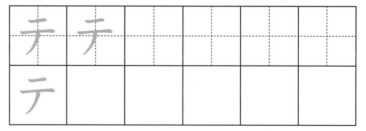

アイウエオ　カキクケコ　サシスセソ　**タチツテト**　ナニヌネノ　ハヒフヘホ　マミムメモ　ヤユヨ　ラリルレロ　ワヲ　ン

To is the right side of a **to**tem pole.

💡 Look at the various forms of this *kana*. Notice what is and is not permissible as variants of the same *kana*.

🔍 Recognize and learn the differences and similarities between the two *kana* in each pair.

	i		*re*		*ri*
					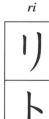
me	*na*		(*shi*)		

✏️ Trace over the model *kana* below carefully. Try to maintain the correct overall shape of the *kana*.

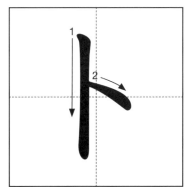

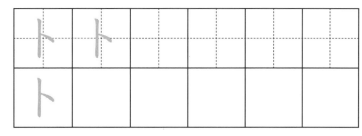

81

アイウエオ カキクケコ サシスセソ タチツテト **ナニヌネノ** ハヒフヘホ マミムメモ ヤユヨ ラリルレロ ワヲ ン

Katakana

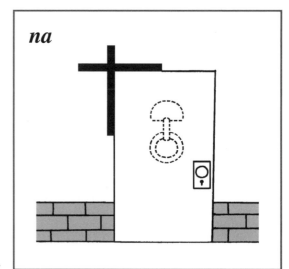

na

Na is a door without a **kno**cker.

💡 Look at the various forms of this *kana*. Notice what is and is not permissible as variants of the same *kana*.

🔍 Recognize and learn the differences and similarities between the two *kana* in each pair.

	chi		*to*		*wa*

me   *i*   *fu*

✏️ Trace over the model *kana* below carefully. Try to maintain the correct overall shape of the *kana*.

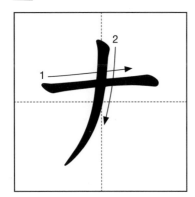 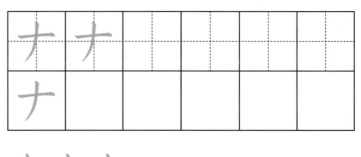

82

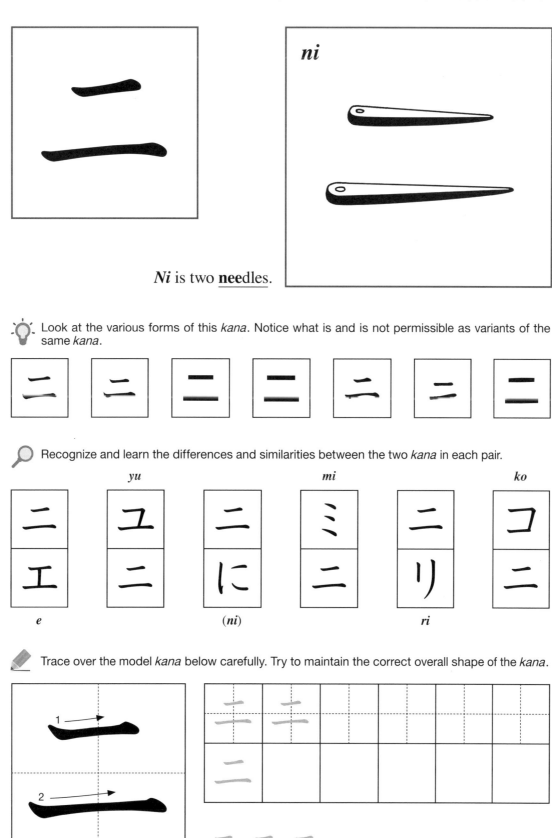

アイウエオ カキクケコ サシスセソ タチツテト **ナニヌネノ** ハヒフヘホ マミムメモ ヤユヨ ラリルレロ ワヲ ン

Katakana

nu

Nu is a **new** sword.

💡 Look at the various forms of this *kana*. Notice what is and is not permissible as variants of the same *kana*.

🔍 Recognize and learn the differences and similarities between the two *kana* in each pair.

	chi		*no*		*ra*
ヌ	チ	ヌ	ノ	ヌ	ラ
タ	ヌ	メ	ヌ	フ	ヌ
ta		*me*		*fu*	

✏️ Trace over the model *kana* below carefully. Try to maintain the correct overall shape of the *kana*.

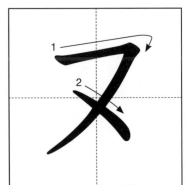

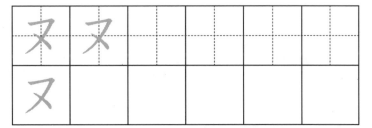

84

アイウエオ カキクケコ サシスセソ タチツテト **ナニヌネノ** ハヒフヘホ マミムメモ ヤユヨ ラリルレロ ワヲ ン

Ne is a bird's **ne**st in a tree.

💡 Look at the various forms of this *kana*. Notice what is and is not permissible as variants of the same *kana*.

🔍 Recognize and learn the differences and similarities between the two *kana* in each pair.

	(*e*)		*o*		*nu*

su		*ho*		*ya*	

✏️ Trace over the model *kana* below carefully. Try to maintain the correct overall shape of the *kana*.

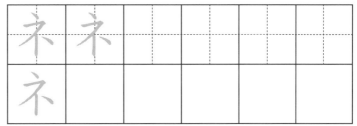

アイウエオ　カキクケコ　サシスセソ　タチツテト　**ナニヌネノ**　ハヒフヘホ　マミムメモ　ヤユヨ　ラリルレロ　ワヲ　ン

Katakana

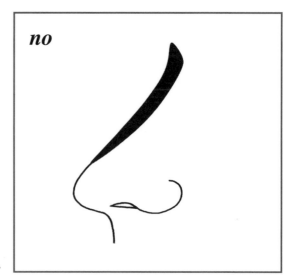

no

No is the bridge of a **no**se.

💡 Look at the various forms of this *kana*. Notice what is and is not permissible as variants of the same *kana*.

🔍 Recognize and learn the differences and similarities between the two *kana* in each pair.

	ri		*re*		*(ku)*

me	*nu*		*(shi)*		

✏️ Trace over the model *kana* below carefully. Try to maintain the correct overall shape of the *kana*.

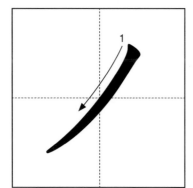

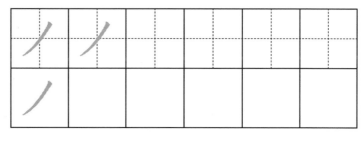

86

アイウエオ　カキクケコ　サシスセソ　タチツテト　ナニヌネノ　**ハヒフヘホ**　マミムメモ　ヤユヨ　ラリルレロ　ワヲ　ン

Ha is a **haw**k laughing "**Ha**-**ha**!"

💡 Look at the various forms of this *kana*. Notice what is and is not permissible as variants of the same *kana*.

🔍 Recognize and learn the differences and similarities between the two *kana* in each pair.

	so		*ri*		*ni*
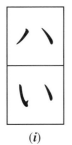		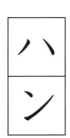			
(*i*)	*n*		*he*		

✏️ Trace over the model *kana* below carefully. Try to maintain the correct overall shape of the *kana*.

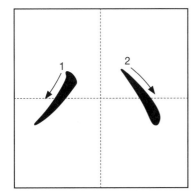
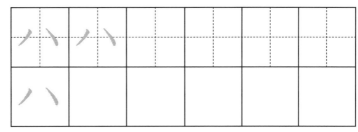

Katakana

アイウエオ カキクケコ サシスセソ タチツテト ナニヌネノ **ハヒフヘホ** マミムメモ ヤユヨ ラリルレロ ワヲ ン

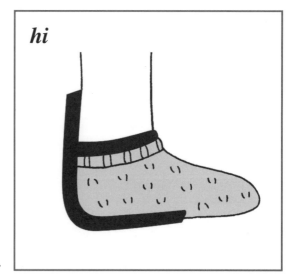

Hi is a **hee**l.

💡 Look at the various forms of this *kana*. Notice what is and is not permissible as variants of the same *kana*.

🔍 Recognize and learn the differences and similarities between the two *kana* in each pair.

	yo		*mo*		(*to*)
ヒ	ヨ	ヒ	モ	ヒ	と
セ	ヒ	ト	ヒ	せ	ヒ
se		*to*		(*se*)	

✏️ Trace over the model *kana* below carefully. Try to maintain the correct overall shape of the *kana*.

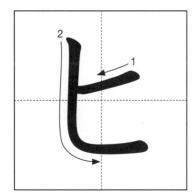

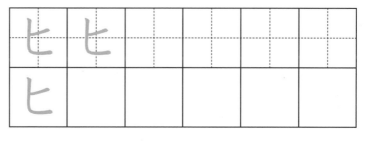

アイウエオ　カキクケコ　サシスセソ　タチツテト　ナニヌネノ　**ハヒフヘホ**　マミムメモ　ヤユヨ　ラリルレロ　ワヲ　ン

fu/hu

Fu/Hu is Little Red Riding **Hoo**d.

💡 Look at the various forms of this *kana*. Notice what is and is not permissible as variants of the same *kana*.

🔍 Recognize and learn the differences and similarities between the two *kana* in each pair.

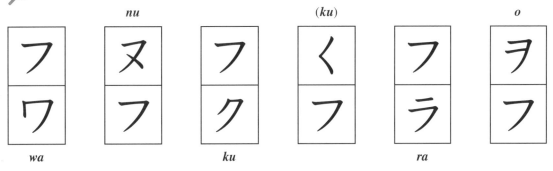

✏️ Trace over the model *kana* below carefully. Try to maintain the correct overall shape of the *kana*.

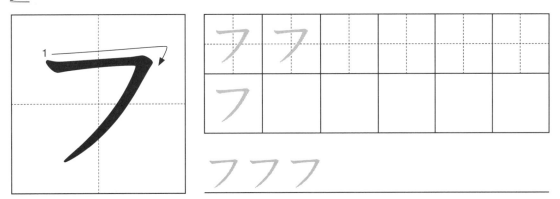

89

アイウエオ カキクケコ サシスセソ タチツテト ナニヌネノ **ハヒフヘホ** マミムメモ ヤユヨ ラリルレロ ワヲ ン

Katakana

He is a **hay**stack.

💡 Look at the various forms of this *kana*. Notice what is and is not permissible as variants of the same *kana*.

🔍 Recognize and learn the differences and similarities between the two *kana* in each pair.

fu		(*tsu*)		*me*
				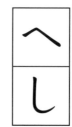	
(*ku*)	*re*		(*shi*)	

✏️ Trace over the model *kana* below carefully. Try to maintain the correct overall shape of the *kana*.

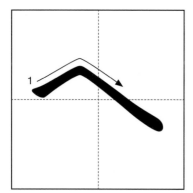

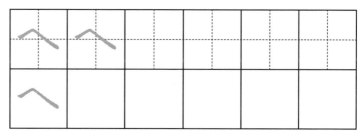

アイウエオ　カキクケコ　サシスセソ　タチツテト　ナニヌネノ　**ハヒフヘホ**　マミムメモ　ヤユヨ　ラリルレロ　ワヲ　ン

ho

Ho is a **ho**ly cross with two people at prayer.

💡 Look at the various forms of this *kana*. Notice what is and is not permissible as variants of the same *kana*.

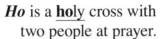

🔍 Recognize and learn the differences and similarities between the two *kana* in each pair.

	ne		*(o)*		*(mu)*
o	*(na)*			*(fu)*	

✏️ Trace over the model *kana* below carefully. Try to maintain the correct overall shape of the *kana*.

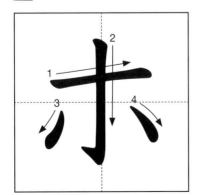

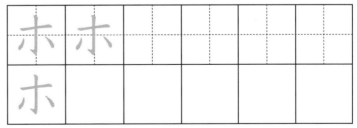

91

Katakana

アイウエオ カキクケコ サシスセソ タチツテト ナニヌネノ ハヒフヘホ **マ**ミムメモ ヤユヨ ラリルレロ ワヲ ン

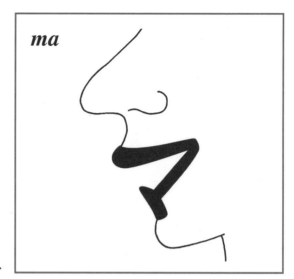

Ma is **ma**ma's **m**outh.

💡 Look at the various forms of this *kana*. Notice what is and is not permissible as variants of the same *kana*.

🔍 Recognize and learn the differences and similarities between the two *kana* in each pair.

	mu		*se*		*(tsu)*
マ	ム	マ	セ	マ	つ
ア	マ	ヤ	マ	ヌ	マ
a		*ya*		*nu*	

✏️ Trace over the model *kana* below carefully. Try to maintain the correct overall shape of the *kana*.

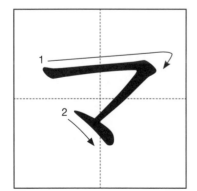

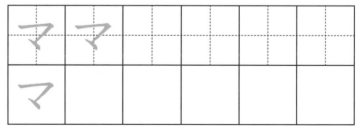

アイウエオ カキクケコ サシスセソ タチツテト ナニヌネノ ハヒフヘホ **マミムメモ** ヤユヨ ラリルレロ ワヲ ン

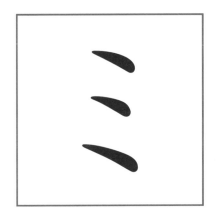

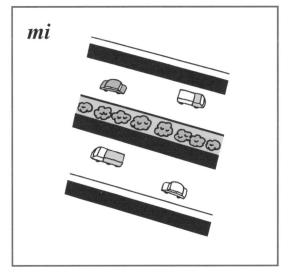

Mi is the **me**dian strip of a highway.

💡 Look at the various forms of this *kana*. Notice what is and is not permissible as variants of the same *kana*.

🔍 Recognize and learn the differences and similarities between the two *kana* in each pair.

	ni		(*ni*)		*te*
		ミ	に	ミ	テ
ヨ		こ		キ	
yo		(*ko*)		*ki*	

✏️ Trace over the model *kana* below carefully. Try to maintain the correct overall shape of the *kana*.

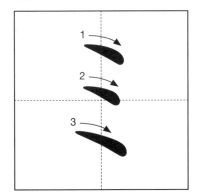

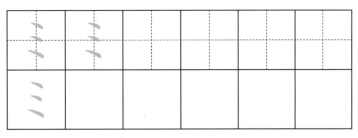

Katakana

アイウエオ カキクケコ サシスセソ タチツテト ナニヌネノ ハヒフヘホ **マミムメモ** ヤユヨ ラリルレロ ワヲ ン

Mu is a **moo**se with huge antlers.

💡 Look at the various forms of this *kana*. Notice what is and is not permissible as variants of the same *kana*.

🔍 Recognize and learn the differences and similarities between the two *kana* in each pair.

	re		*wa*		*nu*
ム	レ	ム	ワ	ム	ヌ
マ	ム	ア	ム	ん	ム
ma		**a**		**(n)**	

✏️ Trace over the model *kana* below carefully. Try to maintain the correct overall shape of the *kana*.

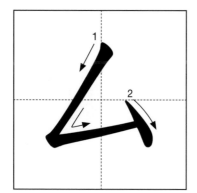

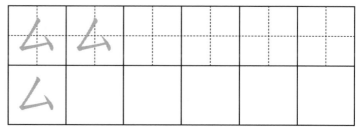

アイウエオ カキクケコ サシスセソ タチツテト ナニヌネノ ハヒフヘホ **マミムメモ** ヤユヨ ラリルレロ ワヲ ン

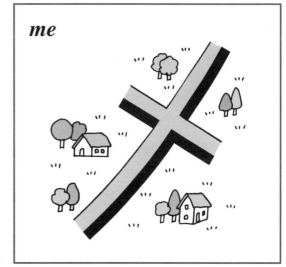
me

Me is two roads that have **me**t.

💡 Look at the various forms of this *kana*. Notice what is and is not permissible as variants of the same *kana*.

🔍 Recognize and learn the differences and similarities between the two *kana* in each pair.

	na		**su**		**no**

nu		**so**		**i**	

✏️ Trace over the model *kana* below carefully. Try to maintain the correct overall shape of the *kana*.

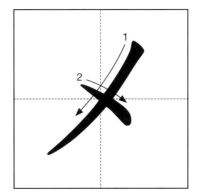

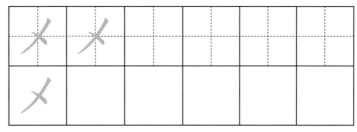

Katakana

アイウエオ カキクケコ サシスセソ タチツテト ナニヌネノ ハヒフヘホ **マミムメモ** ヤユヨ ラリルレロ ワヲ ン

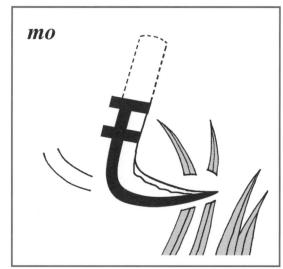

mo

Mo is for **mow**ing grass with a handleless sickle.

💡 Look at the various forms of this *kana*. Notice what is and is not permissible as variants of the same *kana*.

🔍 Recognize and learn the differences and similarities between the two *kana* in each pair.

o		(*ma*)		(*mo*)
te	*se*		*ki*	

✏️ Trace over the model *kana* below carefully. Try to maintain the correct overall shape of the *kana*.

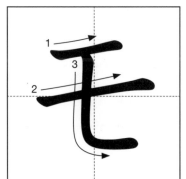

アイウエオ カキクケコ サシスセソ タチツテト ナニヌネノ ハヒフヘホ マミムメモ **ヤユヨ** ラリルレロ ワヲ ン

Ya is the "**Ya**!" Germans say after finishing their beer.

💡 Look at the various forms of this *kana*. Notice what is and is not permissible as variants of the same *kana*.

🔍 Recognize and learn the differences and similarities between the two *kana* in each pair.

	a		*se*		(*ya*)
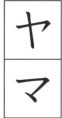				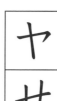	
ma	*ka*			(*se*)	

✏️ Trace over the model *kana* below carefully. Try to maintain the correct overall shape of the *kana*.

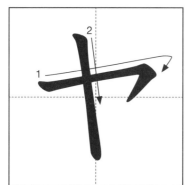

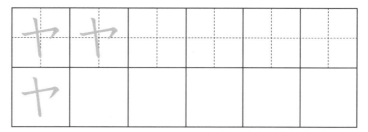

97

アイウエオ カキクケコ サシスセソ タチツテト ナニヌネノ ハヒフヘホ マミムメモ **ヤユヨ** ラリルレロ ワヲ ン

Katakana

yu

Yu is a <u>U</u>-Haul van.

💡 Look at the various forms of this *kana*. Notice what is and is not permissible as variants of the same *kana*.

🔍 Recognize and learn the differences and similarities between the two *kana* in each pair.

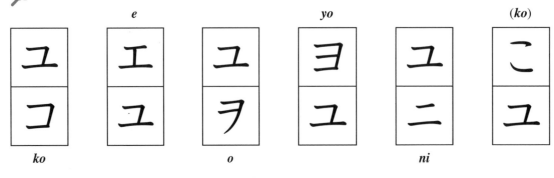

| ko | e | o | yo | ni | (ko) |

✏️ Trace over the model *kana* below carefully. Try to maintain the correct overall shape of the *kana*.

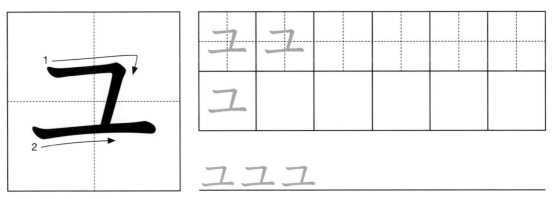

98

アイウエオ カキクケコ サシスセソ タチツテト ナニヌネノ ハヒフヘホ マミムメモ ヤ**ユ**ヨ ラリルレロ ワヲ ン

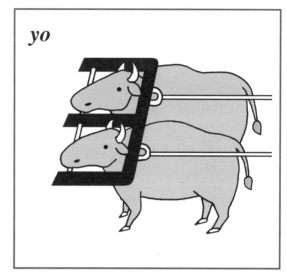

yo

Yo is a **yo**ke on a pair of oxen.

💡 Look at the various forms of this *kana*. Notice what is and is not permissible as variants of the same *kana*.

🔍 Recognize and learn the differences and similarities between the two *kana* in each pair.

	ko		*ta*		*ra*

o   *ni*   *mi*

✏️ Trace over the model *kana* below carefully. Try to maintain the correct overall shape of the *kana*.

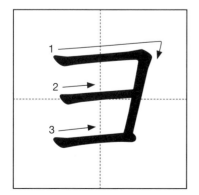

99

Katakana

アイウエオ カキクケコ サシスセソ タチツテト ナニヌネノ ハヒフヘホ マミムメモ ヤユヨ **ラリルレロ** ワヲ ン

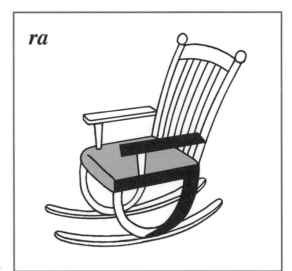

Ra is a **ro**cking chair.

💡 Look at the various forms of this *kana*. Notice what is and is not permissible as variants of the same *kana*.

🔍 Recognize and learn the differences and similarities between the two *kana* in each pair.

	o		*te*		(*u*)
			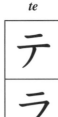		
fu	*wa*		*a*		

✏️ Trace over the model *kana* below carefully. Try to maintain the correct overall shape of the *kana*.

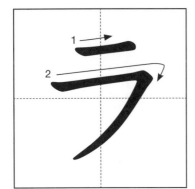

アイウエオ カキクケコ サシスセソ タチツテト ナニヌネノ ハヒフヘホ マミムメモ ヤユヨ **ラリルレロ** ワヲ ン

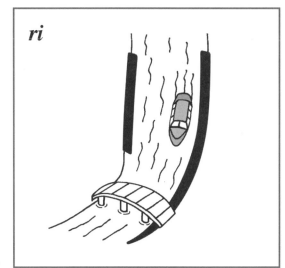

Ri is a **ri**ver.

💡 Look at the various forms of this *kana*. Notice what is and is not permissible as variants of the same *kana*.

🔍 Recognize and learn the differences and similarities between the two *kana* in each pair.

	n		*ha*		*ru*
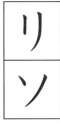		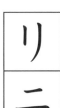			
so		*ni*		*(i)*	

✏️ Trace over the model *kana* below carefully. Try to maintain the correct overall shape of the *kana*.

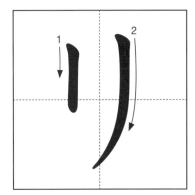

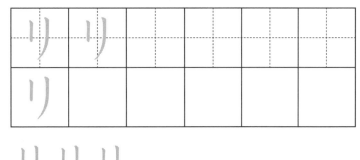

101

アイウエオ　カキクケコ　サシスセソ　タチツテト　ナニヌネノ　ハヒフヘホ　マミムメモ　ヤユヨ　**ラリルレロ**　ワヲ　ン

Katakana

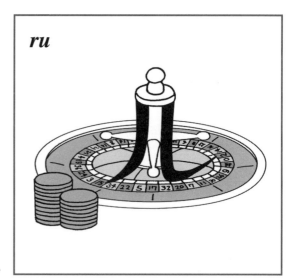

ru

Ru is the spindle of a **rou**lette wheel.

💡 Look at the various forms of this *kana*. Notice what is and is not permissible as variants of the same *kana*.

🔍 Recognize and learn the differences and similarities between the two *kana* in each pair.

	re		*so*		(*i*)
ri	*ha*		*no*		

✏️ Trace over the model *kana* below carefully. Try to maintain the correct overall shape of the *kana*.

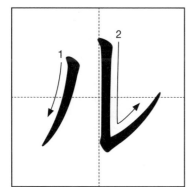

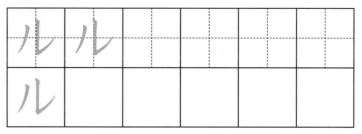

アイウエオ　カキクケコ　サシスセソ　タチツテト　ナニヌネノ　ハヒフヘホ　マミムメモ　ヤユヨ　**ラリル**レ**ロ**　ワヲ　ン

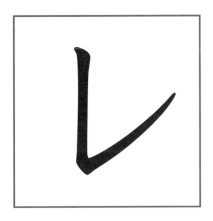

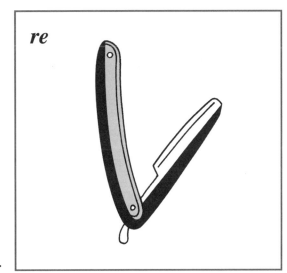

Re is a **ra**zor.

💡 Look at the various forms of this *kana*. Notice what is and is not permissible as variants of the same *kana*.

🔍 Recognize and learn the differences and similarities between the two *kana* in each pair.

	fu		*ru*		*he*

(*shi*)	(*ku*)			*n*	

✏️ Trace over the model *kana* below carefully. Try to maintain the correct overall shape of the *kana*.

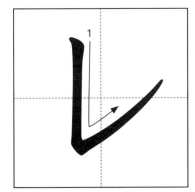

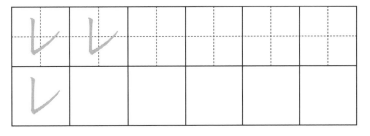

103

アイウエオ　カキクケコ　サシスセソ　タチツテト　ナニヌネノ　ハヒフヘホ　マミムメモ　ヤユヨ　**ラリル レ ロ**　ワヲ　ン

Katakana

Ro is a **ro**bot's head.

💡 Look at the various forms of this *kana*. Notice what is and is not permissible as variants of the same *kana*.

🔍 Recognize and learn the differences and similarities between the two *kana* in each pair.

✏️ Trace over the model *kana* below carefully. Try to maintain the correct overall shape of the *kana*.

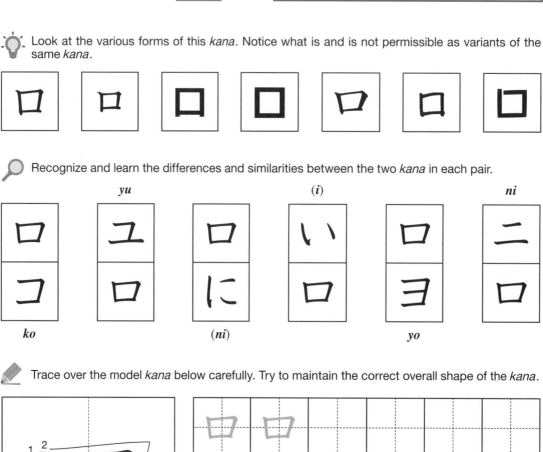

アイウエオ　カキクケコ　サシスセソ　タチツテト　ナニヌネノ　ハヒフヘホ　マミムメモ　ヤユヨ　ラリルレロ　**ワヲ**　ン

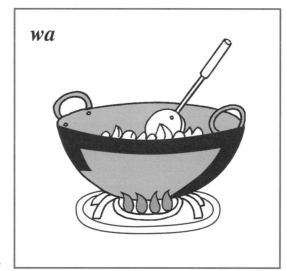

wa

Wa is a <u>wo</u>k, a Chinese cooking pan.

💡 Look at the various forms of this *kana*. Notice what is and is not permissible as variants of the same *kana*.

🔍 Recognize and learn the differences and similarities between the two *kana* in each pair.

	fu		*ya*		*u*
ku		*ra*		*ka*	

✏️ Trace over the model *kana* below carefully. Try to maintain the correct overall shape of the *kana*.

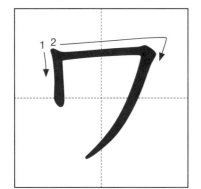

105

アイウエオ　カキクケコ　サシスセソ　タチツテト　ナニヌネノ　ハヒフヘホ　マミムメモ　ヤユヨ　ラリルレロ　**ワヲ**　ン

Katakana

O is an **o**cean liner.

💡 Look at the various forms of this *kana*. Notice what is and is not permissible as variants of the same *kana*.

🔍 Recognize and learn the differences and similarities between the two *kana* in each pair.

fu	*ta*	*wa*
ヲ / フ	ヲ / タ	ヲ / ワ
ラ / ヲ	ヨ / ヲ	ウ / ヲ
ra	*yo*	*u*

✏️ Trace over the model *kana* below carefully. Try to maintain the correct overall shape of the *kana*.

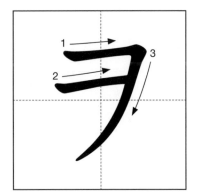

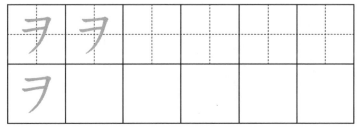

106

アイウエオ　カキクケコ　サシスセソ　タチツテト　ナニヌネノ　ハヒフヘホ　マミムメモ　ヤユヨ　ラリルレロ　ワヲ　ン

N is <u>moun</u><u>tain</u> ridges.

💡 Look at the various forms of this *kana*. Notice what is and is not permissible as variants of the same *kana*.

🔍 Recognize and learn the differences and similarities between the two *kana* in each pair.

	shi		(*ko*)		*ni*
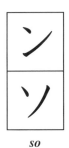		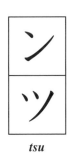		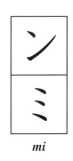	
so		*tsu*		*mi*	

✏️ Trace over the model *kana* below carefully. Try to maintain the correct overall shape of the *kana*.

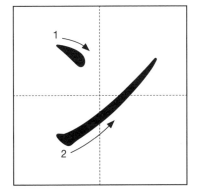
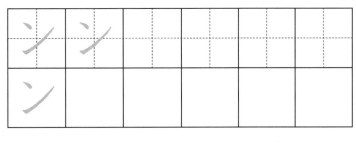

Appendix

I. Elaborations of Basic *Hiragana* and *Katakana*

II. Punctuation Marks

I. Elaborations of Basic *Hiragana* and *Katakana*

1. *Hiragana*

In addition to the basic 46 *hiragana* representing 46 syllables, there are many more characters needed for the other syllables in Japanese. All the other syllables can be represented by slight elaborations of basic *hiragana*.

(1) *Hiragana* with two dots

The four lines of syllables with voiced consonants (for example, English g, z, d and b) are represented by adding two dots at the upper right-hand corner of the corresponding *hiragana*. Due to historical circumstances, *ba-bi-bu-be-bo* syllables are related to *ha-hi-hu-he-ho*.

	a	i	u	e	o
g-	が	ぎ	ぐ	げ	ご
z-	ざ	じ	ず	ぜ	ぞ
d-	だ	ぢ	づ	で	ど
b-	ば	び	ぶ	べ	ぼ

In most cases, じ and ず are used for *ji* and *zu* respectively instead of ぢ and づ. In compounds, the initial syllable of the second word quite commonly receives two dots (or voicing) if the initial syllable is of basic *hiragana*. For example, if such initial syllables are either ち (*chi*) or つ (*tsu*), they become ぢ (*ji*) or づ (*zu*) respectively in compounds, as follows:

はな *hana* + ち *chi* → はなぢ *hanaji*
(nose)   (blood)   (nosebleed)

みか *mika* + つき *tsuki* → みかづき *mikazuki*
(three days)   (moon)   (crescent moon)

Also, after ち and つ, ぢ and づ tend to be used instead of じ and ず respectively.

ちぢむ *chijimu*   つづく *tsuzuku*
(to shrink)   (to continue)

(2) *Hiragana* with a little circle

	a	i	u	e	o
p-	ぱ	ぴ	ぷ	ぺ	ぽ

Pa-pi-pu-pe-po syllables are related to *ha-hi-hu-he-ho* for historical reasons and represented by adding a little circle at the upper right-hand corner of *hiragana* for *ha-hi-hu-he-ho* syllables.

(3) Small や *(ya)* / ゆ *(yu)* / よ *(yo)*

	a	u	o
ky-	きゃ	きゅ	きょ
sh-	しゃ	しゅ	しょ
ch-	ちゃ	ちゅ	ちょ
ny-	にゃ	にゅ	にょ
hy-	ひゃ	ひゅ	ひょ
my-	みゃ	みゅ	みょ
ry-	りゃ	りゅ	りょ
gy-	ぎゃ	ぎゅ	ぎょ
j-	じゃ	じゅ	じょ
by-	びゃ	びゅ	びょ
py-	ぴゃ	ぴゅ	ぴょ

Syllables containing a short "y" sound such as *kya*, *hyo*, or even *shu* (*syu*) are represented by the combination of basic *hiragana* of the *i* column such as き (*ki*), し (*shi*) and ひ (*hi*), and small-sized や (*ya*), ゆ (*yu*) and よ (*yo*). These small や, ゆ and よ are placed in the lower half of a line if they are written horizontally.

If they are written vertically, which is possible in Japanese, they are placed to the right of a column:

きゃ *kya*   みゅ *myu*   ぴょ *pyo*

(4) Long vowels

There are long vowels such as *ā*, *ī*, *ū*, *ē*, and *ō* in Japanese.

The *a* column

Long vowels such as *ā*, *kā*, *sā* and *tā*, i.e., those of the *a* column, are represented by adding あ (*a*) to the first syllable:

  ああ *ā*   かあ *kā*   さあ *sā*   たあ *tā*

The *i* column

Long vowels such as *ī*, *kī*, *chī* and *mī*, i.e., those of the *i* column, are represented by adding い (*i*) to the first syllable:

  いい *ī*   きい *kī*   ちい *chiī*   みい *mī*

The *u* column

Long vowels such as *ū*, *kū*, *sū* and *yū*, i.e., those of the *u* column, are represented by adding う (*u*) to the first syllable:

  うう *ū*   くう *kū*   すう *sū*   ゆう *yū*

The *e* column

Long vowels such as *rē*, *kē*, *sē* and *tē*, i.e., those of the *e* column, are usually represented by adding い (*i*) [not え (*e*)!] to the first syllable:

  れい *rē*   けい *kē*   せい *sē*   てい *tē*

But there are exceptions like the following:

  ええ *ē*   ねえ *nē*   おねえさん *onēsan*
  (yes)   (I say)   (an elder sister)

The *o* column

Long vowels of the *o* column such as *ō*, *kō*, *sō* and *tō* are represented by adding う (*u*) [not お (*o*)!] to the first syllable:

  おう *ō*   こう *kō*   そう *sō*   とう *tō*

But there are some exceptions:

  おおき *ōki*   おおきい *ōkii*   とおい *tōi*   おおい *ōi*
  [surname]   (big)   (far)   (numerous)

  とおり *tōri*   とおる *tōru*   こおる *kōru*
  (street)   (to pass)   (to freeze)

(5) Little つ (tsu)

When two consonants except for *n* are in a row, the first consonant is represented by a little つ (*tsu*) written in the lower half of a horizontal line or to the right of a vertical column:

いっぱい *ippai*　　　みっつ *mittsu*　　　か
　　　　　　　　　　　　　　　　　　　っ *katta*
　　　　　　　　　　　　　　　　　　　た

(6) Particles *wa*, *e* and *o*

The three particles (grammatical markers) in Japanese, *wa* (a topic marker), *e* (a direction marker), and *o* (a direct object marker), are conventionally represented by は (*ha*), へ (*he*) and を (*o*), respectively, due to historical circumstances. は, へ and を are pronounced as *wa*, *e* and *o*, respectively.

わたし は これ を よむ。　　　*Watashi wa kore o yomu.*
とうきょう へ いく。　　　　　*Tōkyō e iku.*

2. Katakana

Most of the modifications applied to *hiragana* can also be applied to *katakana*. Notice one difference between *hiragana* and *katakana* with respect to long vowels.

(1) *Katakana* with two dots

The same as *hiragana*:

	a	i	u	e	o
g-	ガ	ギ	グ	ゲ	ゴ
z-	ザ	ジ	ズ	ゼ	ゾ
d-	ダ	ヂ	ヅ	デ	ド
b-	バ	ビ	ブ	ベ	ボ

(2) *Katakana* with a little circle

The same as *hiragana*:

	a	i	u	e	o
p-	パ	ピ	プ	ペ	ポ

(3) Small ヤ (ya) / ユ (yu) / ヨ (yo)
The same as *hiragana*:

	a	u	o
ky-	キャ	キュ	キョ
sh-	シャ	シュ	ショ
ch-	チャ	チュ	チョ
ny-	ニャ	ニュ	ニョ
hy-	ヒャ	ヒュ	ヒョ
my-	ミャ	ミュ	ミョ
ry-	リャ	リュ	リョ
gy-	ギャ	ギュ	ギョ
j-	ジャ	ジュ	ジョ
by-	ビャ	ビュ	ビョ
py-	ピャ	ピュ	ピョ

(4) Long vowels
In *katakana*, long vowels are always represented by drawing a bar after the first syllable. A horizontal bar is drawn when written horizontally and a vertical bar is used when written vertically:

アー *ā*   キー *kī*   スー *sū*   テー *tē*   ノー *nō*

(5) Little ッ (tsu)
The same as *hiragana*:

コップ *koppu*   ベッド *beddo*

(6) Particles *wa*, *e* and *o*
Since *katakana* are ordinarily reserved for words of foreign origin, Japanese words like grammatical particles are not expressed with *katakana* in ordinary writing. But if special situations necessitate writing all in *katakana*, then these particles are represented just as in *hiragana*:

ワタシ ハ コレ ヲ ヨム。   *Watashi wa kore o yomu.*
トウキョウ ヘ イク。   *Tōkyō e iku.*

II. Punctuation Marks

(1) The small circle
The end of a sentence is marked by a small circle in Japanese. When written horizontally the small circle is placed at the bottom of the line. When written vertically, the small circle is placed to the right of the column.

わたしはいきます。 *Watashi wa ikimasu.*

これはほんです。 *Kore wa hon desu.*

(2) The comma
A comma is used to indicate a pause. The position of the comma is the same as the small circle.

はい、そうです。 *Hai, sō desu.*

(3) Quotation marks
Quotations are indicated by a pair of signs like corners. When written horizontally, the opening sign is placed in the upper half and the closing sign is placed in the lower half, as follows:

「わたしはたなかです。」といいました。

"Watashi wa Tanaka desu." to iimashita.

When written vertically, the opening sign is placed to the right of the column and the closing sign is placed to the left of the column:

「わたしはたなかです。」といいました。

"Watashi wa Tanaka desu." to iimashita.

Hiragana Practice 1   あいうえお かきくけこ

1 Read the following *hiragana*.

(1) え (　　) (2) く (　　) (3) い (　　) (4) け (　　) (5) お (　　)

(6) こ (　　) (7) き (　　) (8) う (　　) (9) か (　　) (10) あ (　　)

2 Time trial: Find the characters in the brackets.

(1) [あ い う え お]

お	ぬ	え	ん
つ	ゆ	あ	て
り	こ	け	い
む	う	く	の

(2) [か き く け こ]

ま	は	し	き
さ	な	ん	て
か	こ	け	い
お	く	に	へ

Your time : ＿＿＿＿＿＿＿＿＿＿　　Your time : ＿＿＿＿＿＿＿＿＿＿

3 Write the following words.

(1) love
a	i

(2) up; above
u	e

(3) voice
ko	e

(4) blue
a	o

(5) red
a	ka

(6) to listen
ki	ku

(7) hill
o	ka

(8) pond
i	ke

Hiragana Practice 2 　さしすせそ たちつてと

1 Read the following *hiragana*.

(1) し (　　) (2) と (　　) (3) た (　　) (4) せ (　　) (5) つ (　　)

(6) そ (　　) (7) ち (　　) (8) さ (　　) (9) て (　　) (10) す (　　)

2 Time trial: Find the characters in the brackets.

(1) [さ し す せ そ]

ろ	も	お	す
よ	さ	く	て
せ	え	け	し
き	ち	そ	や

(2) [た ち つ て と]

と	た	へ	つ
う	な	に	は
ち	ら	け	ん
し	く	て	ろ

Your time : _____　　Your time : _____

3 Write the following words.

(1) sushi

su	shi

(2) sake

sa	ke

(3) world

se	ka	i

(4) outside

so	to

(5) high; expensive

ta	ka	i

(6) subway

chi	ka	te	tsu

Hiragana Practice 3   なにぬねの はひふへほ

1 Read the following *hiragana*.

(1) の (　)　(2) ふ (　)　(3) へ (　)　(4) は (　)　(5) に (　)

(6) ぬ (　)　(7) ほ (　)　(8) な (　)　(9) ね (　)　(10) ひ (　)

2 Time trial: Find the characters in the brackets.

(1) [な に ぬ ね の]

け	に	あ	わ
の	お	は	ゆ
れ	な	た	ね
ゆ	め	こ	ぬ

(2) [は ひ ふ へ ほ]

ろ	ふ	け	き
て	な	や	は
ひ	う	ほ	た
に	つ	へ	と

Your time : _____   Your time : _____

3 Write the following words.

(1) flower

| ha | na |

(2) cloth

| nu | no |

(3) navel

| he | so |

(4) meat

| ni | ku |

(5) bone

| ho | ne |

(6) deep

| fu | ka | i |

(7) airplane

| hi | ko | u | ki |

119

Hiragana Practice 4　まみむめも やゆよ

1 Read the following *hiragana*.

(1) め　(　)　(2) よ　(　)　(3) み　(　)　(4) ま　(　)　(5) ゆ　(　)

(6) も　(　)　(7) や　(　)　(8) む　(　)

2 Time trial: Find the characters in the brackets.

(1) [ま み む め も]

な	お	め	す
む	ほ	き	も
ぬ	お	あ	せ
の	ま	や	み

(2) [や ゆ よ]

め	は	の	き
わ	み	ま	ゆ
よ	す	せ	ぬ
お	や	あ	む

Your time : _____　　　Your time : _____

3 Write the following words.

(1) mountain

ya	ma

(2) to read

yo	mu

(3) dream

yu	me

(4) cloud

ku	mo

(5) paper

ka	mi

(6) daughter

mu	su	me

(7) name

na	ma	e

Hiragana Practice 5 らりるれろ わをん

1 Read the following *hiragana*.

(1) ろ (2) を (3) れ (4) ら (5) ん
( )   ( )   ( )   ( )   ( )

(6) る (7) わ (8) り
( )   ( )   ( )

2 Time trial: Find the characters in the brackets.

(1) [ら り る れ ろ]

お	い	り	う
ら	ゆ	ろ	わ
つ	す	そ	る
ん	れ	ぬ	ち

(2) [わ を ん]

と	へ	を	つ
く	ね	ら	ゆ
わ	ち	そ	れ
ろ	え	ん	お

Your time : _____   Your time : _____

3 Write the following words.

(1) that one

a	re

(2) to understand

wa	ka	ru

(3) to laugh; to smile

wa	ra	u

(4) theory

ri	ro	n

(5) to read books

ho	n	o (wo)	yo	mu

Katakana Practice 1   アイウエオ カキクケコ

イウエオカキケ

1 Read the following *katakana*.

(1) キ (2) イ (3) カ (4) ケ (5) エ
(　) (　) (　) (　) (　)

(6) オ (7) ク (8) ア (9) コ (10) ウ
(　) (　) (　) (　) (　)

2 Time trial: Find the characters in the brackets.

(1) [ア イ ウ エ オ]

フ	ユ	ナ	エ
ア	ウ	メ	コ
メ	テ	マ	ニ
オ	ラ	イ	ノ

(2) [カ キ ク ケ コ]

モ	タ	ヨ	キ
ナ	コ	カ	テ
ケ	ヤ	オ	ニ
リ	チ	ク	ワ

Your time : _____   Your time : _____

3 Write the following words.

(1) air conditioner

e	a	ko	n
			ン

(2) oil

o	i	ru
		ル

(3) cart

ka	(a)	to
	ー	ト

(4) cake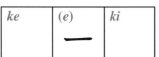

ke	(e)	ki
	ー	

(5) ukulele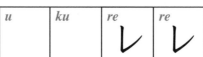

u	ku	re	re
		レ	レ

Katakana Practice 2　サシスセソ タチツテト

1 Read the following *katakana*.

(1) ソ (　)　(2) チ (　)　(3) サ (　)　(4) ト (　)　(5) テ (　)

(6) シ (　)　(7) タ (　)　(8) セ (　)　(9) ツ (　)　(10) ス (　)

2 Time trial: Find the characters in the brackets.

(1) [サ シ ス セ ソ]

ミ	ス	ヤ	マ
メ	ツ	セ	ハ
ソ	サ	ナ	リ
ヌ	ン	ヒ	シ

(2) [タ チ ツ テ ト]

サ	テ	シ	ラ
キ	ク	モ	ト
ツ	イ	レ	チ
ナ	ソ	タ	ヲ

Your time : _____　　　Your time : _____

3 Write the following words.

(1) test

te	su	to

(2) Santa (Claus)

sa	n	ta
	ン	

(3) access

a	ku	se	su

(4) coach

ko	(o)	chi
	ー	

(5) seesaw

shi	(i)	so	(o)
	ー		ー

(6) tour

tsu	a	(a)
		ー

Katakana Practice 3　ナニヌネノ ハヒフヘホ

1 Read the following *katakana*.

(1) ハ (　) (2) ネ (　) (3) ホ (　) (4) ヌ (　) (5) ナ (　)

(6) ヒ (　) (7) ノ (　) (8) ヘ (　) (9) フ (　) (10) ニ (　)

2 Time trial: Find the characters in the brackets.

(1) [ナ ニ ヌ ネ ノ]

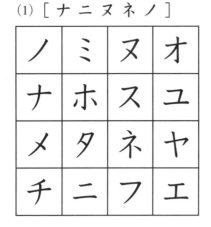

(2) [ハ ヒ フ ヘ ホ]

Your time : _____　　　Your time : _____

3 Write the following words.

(1) knife

na	i	fu

(2) healthy

he	ru	shi	(i)
	ル		一

(3) canoe

ka	nu	(u)
		一

(4) hotel

ho	te	ru
		ル

(5) necktie

ne	ku	ta	i

(6) note

no	(o)	to
	一	

(7) high heels

ha	i	hi	(i)	ru
			一	ル

(8) tennis

te	ni	su

Katakana Practice 4 　マミムメモ ヤユヨ

1 Read the following *katakana*.

(1) ユ　　(2) ミ　　(3) マ　　(4) ヤ　　(5) モ
(　)　　(　)　　(　)　　(　)　　(　)

(6) メ　　(7) ヨ　　(8) ム
(　)　　(　)　　(　)

2 Time trial: Find the characters in the brackets.

(1) [マ ミ ム メ モ]

テ	モ	ナ	ヌ
ミ	ヤ	レ	ム
キ	ニ	ア	ヨ
セ	マ	ヲ	メ

Your time : ＿＿＿＿＿＿＿＿＿

(2) [ヤ ユ ヨ]

ヲ	ミ	タ	ラ
セ	マ	ヤ	ヨ
ユ	カ	ア	コ
セ	エ	ヤ	マ

Your time : ＿＿＿＿＿＿＿＿＿

3 Write the following words.

(1) memo

me	mo

(2) tire

ta	i	ya

(3) crayon

ku	re	yo	n
	レ		ン

(4) ham

ha	mu

(5) Miami

ma	i	a	mi

(6) euro

yu	(u)	ro
	一	ロ

125

Katakana Practice 5   ラリルレロ ワヲン

1 Read the following *katakana*.

(1) ル (　　)　(2) ワ (　　)　(3) ラ (　　)　(4) ン (　　)　(5) ヲ (　　)

(6) リ (　　)　(7) ロ (　　)　(8) レ (　　)

2 Time trial: Find the characters in the brackets.

(1) [ラ リ ル レ ロ]

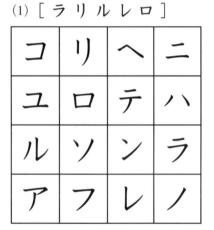

(2) [ワ ヲ ン]

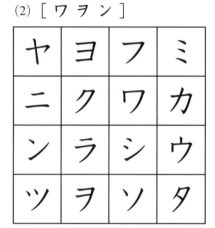

Your time : ＿＿＿＿　　　　Your time : ＿＿＿＿

3 Write the following words.

(1) restaurant

re	su	to	ra	n

(2) calorie

ka	ro	ri	(i)
			ー

(3) wine

wa	i	n

(4) flute

fu	ru	(u)	to
		ー	

Answers

Hiragana Practice 1

1 (1) *e* (2) *ku* (3) *i* (4) *ke* (5) *o*
(6) *ko* (7) *ki* (8) *u* (9) *ka* (10) *a*

3 (1) あい (2) うえ (3) こえ (4) あお
(5) あか (6) きく (7) おか (8) いけ

2 (1)

お	ぬ	え	ん
つ	ゆ	あ	て
り	こ	け	い
む	う	く	の

(2)

ま	は	し	き
さ	な	ん	て
か	こ	け	い
お	く	に	へ

Hiragana Practice 2

1 (1) *shi* (2) *to* (3) *ta* (4) *se* (5) *tsu*
(6) *so* (7) *chi* (8) *sa* (9) *te* (10) *su*

3 (1) すし (2) さけ (3) せかい
(4) そと (5) たかい (6) ちかてつ

2 (1)

ろ	も	お	す
よ	さ	く	て
せ	え	け	し
き	ち	そ	や

(2)

と	た	へ	つ
う	な	に	は
ち	ら	け	ん
し	く	て	ろ

Hiragana Practice 3

1 (1) *no* (2) *fu* (3) *he* (4) *ha* (5) *ni*
(6) *nu* (7) *ho* (8) *na* (9) *ne* (10) *hi*

3 (1) はな (2) ぬの (3) へそ (4) にく
(5) ほね (6) ふかい (7) ひこうき

2 (1)

け	に	あ	わ
の	お	は	ゆ
れ	な	た	ね
ゆ	め	こ	ぬ

(2)

ろ	ふ	け	き
て	な	や	は
ひ	う	ほ	た
に	つ	へ	と

Hiragana Practice 4

1 (1) *me* (2) *yo* (3) *mi* (4) *ma* (5) *yu*
(6) *mo* (7) *ya* (8) *mu*

3 (1) やま (2) よむ (3) ゆめ (4) くも
(5) かみ (6) むすめ (7) なまえ

2 (1)

な	お	め	す
む	ほ	き	も
ぬ	お	あ	せ
の	ま	や	み

(2)

め	は	の	き
わ	み	ま	ゆ
よ	す	せ	ぬ
お	や	あ	む

Hiragana Practice 5

1 (1) *ro* (2) *o* (3) *re* (4) *ra* (5) *n*
(6) *ru* (7) *wa* (8) *ri*

3 (1) あれ (2) わかる (3) わらう
(4) りろん (5) ほんをよむ

2 (1)

お	い	り	う
ら	ゆ	ろ	わ
つ	す	そ	る
ん	れ	ぬ	ち

(2)

と	へ	を	つ
く	ね	ら	ゆ
わ	ち	そ	れ
ろ	え	ん	お

Katakana Practice 1

1 (1) *ki* (2) *i* (3) *ka* (4) *ke* (5) *e*
(6) *o* (7) *ku* (8) *a* (9) *ko* (10) *u*

3 (1) エアコ（ン） (2) オイ（ル） (3) カ（ー）ト
(4) ケ（ー）キ (5) ウク（レレ）

2 (1)

フ	ユ	ナ	エ
ア	ウ	メ	コ
メ	テ	マ	ニ
オ	ラ	イ	ノ

(2)

モ	タ	ヨ	キ
ナ	コ	カ	テ
ケ	ヤ	オ	ニ
リ	チ	ク	ワ

Katakana Practice 2

1 (1) *so* (2) *chi* (3) *sa* (4) *to* (5) *te*
(6) *shi* (7) *ta* (8) *se* (9) *tsu* (10) *su*

3 (1) テスト (2) サ（ン）タ (3) アクセス
(4) コ（ー）チ (5) シ（ー）ソ（ー）
(6) ツア（ー）

2 (1)

ミ	ス	ヤ	マ
メ	ツ	セ	ハ
ソ	サ	ナ	リ
ヌ	ン	ヒ	シ

(2)

サ	テ	シ	ラ
キ	ク	モ	ト
ツ	イ	レ	チ
ナ	ソ	タ	ヲ

Katakana Practice 3

1 (1) *ha* (2) *ne* (3) *ho* (4) *nu* (5) *na*
(6) *hi* (7) *no* (8) *he* (9) *fu* (10) *ni*

3 (1) ナイフ (2) ヘ（ル）シ（ー） (3) カヌ（ー）
(4) ホテ（ル） (5) ネクタイ (6) ノ（ー）ト
(7) ハイヒ（ール） (8) テニス

2 (1)

ノ	ミ	ヌ	オ
ナ	ホ	ス	ユ
メ	タ	ネ	ヤ
チ	ニ	フ	エ

(2)

モ	ヒ	ン	ヲ
リ	ク	ハ	ワ
ホ	レ	セ	ヘ
オ	フ	ソ	ネ

Katakana Practice 4

1 (1) *yu* (2) *mi* (3) *ma* (4) *ya* (5) *mo*
(6) *me* (7) *yo* (8) *mu*

3 (1) メモ (2) タイヤ (3) ク（レ）ヨ（ン）
(4) ハム (5) マイアミ (6) ユ（ーロ）

2 (1)

テ	モ	ナ	ヌ
ミ	ヤ	レ	ム
キ	ニ	ア	ヨ
セ	マ	ヲ	メ

(2)

ヲ	ミ	タ	ラ
セ	マ	や	ヨ
ユ	カ	ア	コ
セ	エ	ヤ	マ

Katakana Practice 5

1 (1) *ru* (2) *wa* (3) *ra* (4) *n* (5) *o*
(6) *ri* (7) *ro* (8) *re*

3 (1) レストラン (2) カロリ（ー）
(3) ワイン (4) フル（ー）ト

2 (1)

コ	リ	ヘ	ニ
ユ	ロ	テ	ハ
ル	ソ	ン	ラ
ア	フ	レ	ノ

(2)

ヤ	ヨ	フ	ミ
ニ	ク	ワ	カ
ン	ラ	シ	ウ
ツ	ヲ	ソ	タ

Katakana